Sport, Ethics and Education

Peter J. Arnold

CASSELL

Cassell
Wellington House
125 Strand
London WC2R 0BB

PO Box 605
Herndon
VA 20172

First Published 1997

British Library Cataloguing-in-Publication Data
A catalogue record for this book is available from the British Library.

ISBN 0–304–70000–2 (hardback)
      0–304–70001–0 (paperback)

Typeset by ensystems, Cambridge
Printed and bound in Great Britain by Redwood Books, Trowbridge, Wiltshire

Also available from Cassell:

N. Armstrong (ed.): *New Directions in Physical Education*
H. Silver: *Good Schools, Effective Schools*
P. Dalin and V. D. Rust: *Towards Schooling for the Twenty First Century*
M. Barber and R. Dann (eds): *Raising Educational Standards in the Inner Cities*
L. Cantor, I. Roberts and B. Pratley: *A Guide to Further Education in England and Wales*
J. Avis, M. Bloomer, G. Esland, D. Gleeson and P. Hodkinson: *Knowledge and Nationhood*
A. Stables: *Subjects of Choice*
D. H. Thomas (ed.): *Flexible Learning Strategies in Higher and Further Education*

Contents

Foreword

Dr Arnold says in the Introduction to this book '... although sport is an important institutional activity which affects our social, economic and political lives, it has increasingly over the past few years been brought into disrepute. Aggression, violence, cheating and drug-taking are some of the unsavoury forms of behaviour that have afflicted its conduct.' I wrote in 1995, 'In earlier, more innocent times, sport in schools was considered a vehicle for inculcating such virtues as honesty, perseverance, humility, and courage, to name a few. The rhetoric espousing these values was a major ideological commitment in physical education. However, recently, greater sophistication in psychological, sociological, historical, and philosophical research has raised serious questions about the validity of these earlier value assertions about school sports.'

In the past few decades the ethics of sport has become a 'hot' topic, partly because of the extremes mentioned above which have alarmed many people connected with sport. The Philosophic Society for the Study of Sport in its conferences and in the *Journal of the Philosophy of Sport* regularly discusses ethical concerns; several books on sport ethics have been published; some conferences with exclusive focus on the ethics of sport have convened; in Canada the Commission on Fair Play has developed elementary school units; and some intercollegiate sports leagues in the USA have promulgated regulations on ethics. This book, *Sport, Ethics and Education*, is welcomed as a unique and promising contribution to efforts to cope with the apparent degeneration of sport.

A fundamental and clearly relevant source for a normative ethic for sport is a definitive conception of what sport ought to be. Such a conception needs to go beyond a sociological description of what now happens in sport. To provide this conception Dr Arnold offers compelling arguments for understanding sport as a 'valued human practice'. Following Alasdair MacIntyre in *After Virtue*, Arnold says '... sport is a practice because it is a peculiarly human activity in which values internal to that activity are discovered and realized in the course of trying to achieve the standards of excellence that characterize it.' Accordingly, to identify how sports participants ought and ought not to act in ethically right ways requires an explication of sport as a practice. Further, an understanding of sport as a practice can readily be translated into consistent guides for ethically right actions.

Arnold informs us that sport understood as a practice has its own integrity governed by its rules and ethos. While some of the particulars of the rules and ethos may change through history, they are not so elastic that no reasonable boundaries are set. Indeed, the rules of sport are inherently based upon the moral concepts of justice and equality. Thus, if a sport established a rule which negated each participant's equal opportunity to perform at his/her best, it would be contradictory to the inherent nature of sport as a practice. For instance, if one tennis player, by rule, was allowed three chances to get the serve in court while the other was allowed two chances, it would contravene equality. And further, if one basketball player, by rule, was awarded two foul shots for the same violation as an opponent, who was awarded one foul shot, then injustice would occur. From such examples it is easy to see that most sports rules attempt to adhere to justice and equality.

Sport as a practice is also governed by an ethos reflective of high ideals and cherished traditions. For instance, it is the case even in high stakes, world-class tennis that linesmen's errors that are detrimental to the earned achievement of a player are sometimes questioned by an opponent who becomes advantaged by such an error. It is also the case that professional golfers will assess a penalty stroke on themselves if, upon address, the ball moves, even though no one else could see it. Such actions are in accord with the best in the ideals and traditions of these sports. While it is a fact that such ideals and traditions are sometimes neglected, it is also the case that such neglect becomes highlighted, and negatively viewed, because of the existence of the ideals and traditions. Sports participants who understand sport as a valued human practice know that pursuing the excellence of the sport itself requires exercise of the virtues of courage, honesty, and justice to facilitate that excellence. At times acting in accord with such virtues results in reducing a competitor's opportunity to win but maintains the integrity of the sport itself, a result which is positive for all. When sports participants see one another, with respect, as mutual guardians of the integrity of sport, the atmosphere becomes one of generosity and friendly engagement and this facilitates a desirable quality in human relationships.

In explicating sport as a valued practice in the ways briefly described above, Dr Arnold shows us that it is an inherently moral practice. In schools, then, the effort to teach and coach sport as such a practice develops the virtues needed to sustain integrity of the practice, provides experience in the exercise of such virtues, and, by so doing, reinforces them. It becomes a process which is focused on sport as moral practice and teaches sport as sport, not as a vehicle for something external to itself. In this way instruction in sport as a practice contributes to moral education, but without using sport as an instrument. When schools and colleges comprehend this they will know clearly that the use of sport for economic ends, for institutional prestige or for entertainment of the public are secondary and that such primary emphases in the organization and administration of sport compromise its moral integrity.

Finally, Dr Arnold makes the case for sport as a part of liberal education in a democracy. Initiation into sport as a valued human practice contributes to practical reasoning (the ability to do something in the world). Knowing how to participate in worthwhile sport is an important aspect of human development. Arnold informs us that such development is valuable in liberal education because practices such as sport (1) '... help constitute a meaningful pattern of life in which individuals can both find and extend themselves.' (2) '... provide the means by which individuals become persons. It is only by being initiated into the ways, customs and practices of a given culture that individuals become the people they are.' (3) '... are indispensable to moral life for without them there would be little need for the cooperative endeavours and the personal virtues they demand.' (4) as '... intrinsically valuable practices ... are important to education because they constitute what is worthwhile in a society and should be passed on to the next generation.'

Sport, Ethics and Education makes a most valuable, as well as unique, contribution to the literature on the ethics of sport. Because of its clear delineation of sport as a valued cultural practice which, when so understood, is inherently moral, it establishes a solid foundation for sport as an important element in the liberal education of individuals in a democracy. Sport is to be taught and comprehended as a liberating practice which requires the exercise of moral virtues in pursuit of the internal goods of sport.

Warren P. Fraleigh
State University of New York, College at Brockport
October 1996

Acknowledgements

In thinking about the present it is easy to forget those many people in the past who have helped shape my ideas. In this respect I would like to thank those former tutors, colleagues and students who perhaps unknowingly have assisted in the formulation of this book.

I would like to thank also my fellow members and friends in The Philosophic Society for the Study of Sport for their comment and conviviality. It was in Boston in 1972 that this society was born and since that time it has established itself as a healthy if relatively small body of international scholars concerned with sport as a distinctive focus of study. It has been a pleasure for me to meet annually with kindred spirits and to enter into dialogue with them on topics of common interest. The sharpening of my thoughts either directly or indirectly in the case of this book owes a lot to meeting with such members as Warren Fraleigh, Earle Zeigler, David Fairchild, Scott Kretchmar, Bill Morgan, Bob Osterhoudt, Gunner Breivik, Sigmund Loland, Sharon Stoll and Angela Schneider. It is particularly pleasing to me that the first named, a founder member of the society and one of its first Presidents, has agreed to write the Foreword to this volume.

In view of the above it will come perhaps as something of a surprise to learn that it is to Alasdair MacIntyre – alas not a society member – who, more than any other philosopher, helped provide me by his explication of what a 'practice' is with a conceptual framework of what I wanted to say. It was through his writings that I came to see that sport, its meaning and moral implications, is best understood as a valued human practice. To him, therefore, I am indebted even though what I have written may not be altogether faithful to what he himself might have written on the subject.

A further source of inspiration for writing this book came as a result of spending some ten days at ancient Olympia at the invitation of the International Olympic Academy in 1995, in order to lecture to and hold seminars with educationists and staff from Institutes of Higher Education from all over the world on issues concerning Olympism. The seminars proved fertile and productive. Some involved the manifold issues confronting international sport and the need for a universal ethic of sport that

xii *Acknowledgements*

all cultures can accept. *Sport, Ethics and Education* can in many respects be regarded as an attempt to make coherent many of the ideas and sentiments expressed in the different types of session that were held. To all the participants and organizers and especially to Freddy Serpieris and Konstantinos Georgiadis I owe a considerable debt.

Several chapters of the book are revised, modified and/or extended versions of previously published articles and I would like to thank the following journals for permission to use some of that material in this volume: *Journal of the Philosophy of Education*, *The Journal of Moral Education*, *Journal of the Philosophy of Sport*, and *Quest*.

My thanks must go also to Gordon Kirk, Principal of Moray House Institute of Education, for making it possible in a climate of stringency to get some help with the practical business of word processing and duplication. Finally I would like to thank my wife Jane who has helped in the completion of this book in a variety of ways.

Peter Arnold
Edinburgh, September 1996

Introduction

In a recent governmental initiative, the Prime Minister of the United Kingdom, John Major, has said that he wishes 'to put sport back at the heart of weekly life in every school' and to re-establish it as 'one of the great pillars of education alongside the academic, the vocational and the moral'.[1] This is welcome news to educationists like myself who have seen not only a decline of the place of sport in recent years as an aspect of school life but also as an element in the physical education programme. What is important about this new initiative is that it sees the school as the point at which the development of sport for the nation as a whole must begin. It recognizes, furthermore, that if sport and the benefits that can flow from it are to flourish, it must not only be taught effectively but also be adequately funded and supported at all levels of endeavour.

What might have been more clearly expressed in this document, however, like so many others concerned with the place of sport in education and society, is that sport can only be properly conducted, especially from the moral point of view, if it is adequately understood. This not only includes the notion of 'fair play' but a good deal more besides. It is because the ethical basis of sport is often referred to but rarely elaborated upon that I have attempted to spell out and make more explicit what this involves, so that teachers, players and officials alike can benefit.

It is hoped that the outcome will not only be a contribution to the study of sport but also to what is pedagogically necessary in the teaching of it, at whatever level that may be. What should be emphasized is that ethical issues in and about sport are not only a British problem but a worldwide one. This book will be of interest, therefore, not only to educators but also to all people regardless of their sex, race, colour, language, religion or political affiliation, who are concerned with the promotion and welfare of sport and who see in it an opportunity for human achievement and accord.

The aims of *Sport, Ethics and Education* are twofold. The first is to argue that sport is best understood as a valued human practice which is inherently concerned with the moral. The second is to argue that sport in the context of the school, no matter what other purposes it may also serve, is or should be a form of moral education. Why is such a book needed now? There are at least two answers to this question. The first is that although sport is an important institutional activity which affects our social, economic and political lives, it has increasingly over the past few years been brought into disrepute. Aggression, violence, cheating and drug-taking are some of the unsavoury forms of behaviour that have afflicted its conduct. It is desirable, therefore, that an attempt should be made to reverse this trend. Bad behaviour in sport is occasionally explained, if not excused, by the 'mirror of life' view of sport, which maintains that what goes on in sport is but a reflection of what goes on in society, with the implication that nothing much can be done about it. This, however, need not be the case. The fact is that if sport is to remain a worthwhile element in our lives it is necessary that it should be practised in accordance with its ideals and best traditions. The second answer is that unless the concept and practice of sport is made clear from the social and moral point of view there is little chance of its teachers, participants, officials, administrators and fans developing appropriate attitudes, judgements and conduct towards it. There is then the need for a well-delineated and understood picture of what sport is and what it entails. The 'practice view of sport', as I call it, provides such a picture. It gives those interested in the welfare of sport a moral reference point by which it can be checked and the actions associated with it appraised. At the heart of sport, it is argued, are ethical principles, virtues and inter-personal concerns, the nature and extent of which are not always fully understood and appreciated.

Sport, Ethics and Education sets out not only to make the ethical basis of sport clear but also to provide teachers, coaches and organizers with a normative framework within which sport should be taught and practised. This is not only necessary if it is to preserve its own intrinsic values and standards but also if it is to resist the external pressures coming from society in the form of power, status, prestige and money which threaten to undermine and corrupt it. Sport should not so much be seen as a microcosm of society but as an exemplification of the good life – a life in which people come together in pursuit of particular goods and forms of excellence.

An outline of the book is as follows. Chapter 1 provides a background understanding of the ones that follow. It argues that the practice of sport, as distinct from its institutionalization, is now best seen as a result of its globalization in terms of universalism rather than in terms of relativisim. This is upheld not only in the light of its common concepts and skills but also in the light of its common ethical principles and characterizing virtues. It is argued also that if sport is to be justified as a part of the educational curriculum in schools, it is necessary that pupils throughout the world be initiated into it in such a way that it is pursued for its own intrinsic values rather than used as an instrument for purposes, good or bad, that are external to it.

Chapter 2 argues that sport is a valued human practice and suggests that, like the law or medicine, it is characterized as much by the moral manner in which its participants conduct themselves as by the pursuit of its own skills, standards and excellences. Virtues, such as justice, honesty and courage are not only necessary to pursue its goals but to protect it from being corrupted by external interests. It is in having as its prime concern the pursuit of its own internal goals rather than extrinsic ones that largely differentiates the practice or prescriptive view of sport from what I have called the sociological or descriptive view.

Chapter 3 is devoted to explicating how the practice view of sport provides a moral basis for the consideration of moral issues that arise in sport. The syndrome of 'winning at all costs', it is argued, exemplifies a state of mind that is antithetical to sport as a culturally valued practice. It signifies a call for victory, without a corresponding concern for sport's internal values or the moral manner in which it should be conducted. The question of the taking of performance-enhancing drugs in sport is discussed and three moral arguments are presented to show that they not only break the rules of sport but offend the very principles and ethos upon which sport as a valued human practice is based.

Chapter 4 looks quite specifically at the nature of competition and its relationship to education and sport. Two critiques of sport as a competitive activity are presented and then discussed with reference to education and the role of the teacher.

Chapter 5 takes up the long-standing belief that there is a connection between a person's physical life and the development and formation of his or her character. After looking at the relationship between education and the notion of having a character, it is argued, in spite of the absence of much clearcut supportive empirical evidence, that there is a necessary or logical relationship between the notion of sport as fairness and the development of a moral character. It is argued further that there are not many situations in life that provide the kind or number of opportunities that call into play the qualities and virtues that are generally considered desirable and that sport both offers and demands.

Chapter 6 gets to the heart of what is involved in the practice view of sport. It argues that sport without the notion of sportsmanship (sportspersonship), especially from the social and moral points of view, leaves it somewhat impoverished. Sports-personship, it is suggested, is not just a term of approval to do with acts in accordance with what is fair. This is something that should be expected of all contestants. Rather it is multidimensional in nature, involving such phenomena as camaraderie, generosity and magnanimity, as well as care and concern for others. It is suggested that sportspersonship as a form of altruism helps characterize what it is to be morally educated.

Chapter 7 provides not only a summary and overview of the preceding chapters but makes more explicit what moral education is and how the practice view of sport relates to it. The chapter starts by outlining three views of sport in relation to the moral life and then goes on to spell out what sorts of consideration underpin the meaning and practice of morality and moral education. The moral basis of an education in sport is then presented. Such processes as judging, caring and acting are seen to be important. The role of the teacher is then discussed before concluding that the moral manifestations of a successful initiation into sport as a valued human practice are those of the display of fairness, character and sportspersonship.

Finally, Chapter 8 places what has been previously said in the wider context of a liberal education and democracy. It argues that democracy should not only be seen in terms of political institutions but also in terms of the quality of individual and social life of which sport is a part. Such principles as freedom and equality are not only the bedrock of a democratic society but constitute the means by which it is evaluated. Education, although concerned with the development of rational and moral agents which are important to democracy should not, however, be seen as a tool of democracy but rather as a condition of its survival. It is suggested further that if education is seen only as the cultivation of the intellect or as a means in the preparation for work, it will leave the growing individual and future citizen somewhat impoverished as a person. Sport, it is argued, is an important element in our culture and should be included as a necessary element in a modern liberal education. It helps provide a reasonable balance of what is worthwhile in life and living. Sport, like other valued pursuits, has its own intrinsic values and standards and demands that these should be appreciated for what they are. Finally, it is argued that sport is the kind of activity that should feature as part of government policy not only on grounds of citizens' rights but also on grounds of its possible outcome in terms of health and social welfare.

Sport, Ethics and Education is a book that is distinctive on two main grounds. First, it is the only book that I know of to examine philosophically the relationship between sport and education from the social and moral point of view. Second, by presenting sport as an ethically based and valued cultural practice in which the moral is an intrinsic and necessary part of the meeting of its own ends and purposes, it offers an evaluative account of sport by means of which judgements about what is appropriate conduct in sport can be more easily made. The book will, therefore, be of theoretical and practical interest to teachers, officials, administrators and sports lovers alike. Its subject matter and content is of international concern and I would expect it to be sold not only to educational establishments throughout the world – to schools, colleges, universities, where there is a wish to promote sport in an educationally justifiable way – but in particular to those people who have a special responsibility for the professional preparation of teachers, coaches and recreational leaders. It will also be of interest to those who teach philosophy and the philosophy of sport as a topic in liberal arts programmes. Finally, it will be of interest to those large organizations such as the International Olympic Academy whose mission it is to proselytize sport as a form of goodwill and understanding between all peoples, cultures and nations.

NOTE

1. Introductory letter in: *Sport: Raising the Game.* London: Department of Heritage, 1995.

Chapter 1

Sport, Universalism and Education

The purpose of this chapter is to provide a background understanding for the ones that follow. Three things will be argued: first, that sport is now a global phenomenon and is best understood as a trans-cultural valued human practice; second, that this view of sport, despite its corruption from time to time, is inherently concerned with concepts, ethical principles and moral values which are universally applicable; and third, that if sport is to be taught and justified as a form of education it should be pursued for its own intrinsic worth rather than for those extrinsic values or purposes that are often associated with it.

SPORT AS A TRANS-CULTURAL UNIVERSAL PRACTICE

Sport today is a universal phenomenon. It is represented in all five continents and almost 200 nations compete in the Olympic Games. Such events as World Cup athletics, soccer or rugby, command global television audiences and vast sums of money are paid to bring them before an ever-growing public eager to see how their team plays and what results it can achieve. In a recent report on American Attitudes towards sport,[1] which was one of the most extensive ever undertaken, it was found that some 96.3 per cent of the population plays, watches or reads about sports with some frequency or identifies with particular teams or players. It was found, furthermore, that almost 70 per cent follow sports every day and that 42 per cent participate in some form of activity daily. These findings may be, of course, peculiar to American society, but few can doubt that sport, wherever it is engaged in, is an important and pervasive influence in the contemporary world. Such is its impact, wrote Boyle (1963, pp. 3–4), that 'it touches upon and deeply influences such disparate elements as status, race relations, business life, automobile design, clothing styles, the concept of the hero, language and ethical values'. The demand and appetite for sport, whether it is played well or badly, whether done for reward or intrinsic satisfaction, has become for many people, according to Leonard (1993, p. 21), something of an opiate which helps take away the pain and strain of boring and frustrating work.

In the foreseeable future it is likely that the place and influence of sport will continue to grow. Few people, however, so far have expressed concern about the integrity of that growth. While it is likely that most 'low level' sport can be considered beneficial in some way to both the individual and society, it is by no means necessarily the case with 'high level' sport, especially perhaps when done professionally and where rewards of various kinds are linked to results. What sport lovers and educators alike should be increasingly vigilant about is the abuse or degradation of sport. Morgan (1994, p. 1) helps identify what is being referred to here. He writes that:

> the mania for winning, the widespread cheating, the economic and political trivialisation of sport, the thirst for crude sensationalism and eccentric spectacle, the manipulation by the mass media, the cult of athletic stars and celebrity, and the mindless bureaucratisation are just some of the ominous signs.

With the universalism and growing pervasiveness of sport in everyday life it would seem there has at the same time been a corresponding increase in its malaise. If this is so, what if anything can be done about it?

Before attempting to answer this question, it will be helpful to differentiate between 'sport as a practice' and 'sport as an institution'. What the relationship is between the two terms and how they differ from one another will be elaborated upon later. For the present it is sufficient to note, following MacIntyre (1985, p. 131), that whereas a practice is a special kind of rule-governed activity which is characterized by the internal goals and standards that make it up, an institution is concerned also and necessarily with the promotion of such external goals as power, status, prestige and money.[2] Whereas the practice of sport is concerned only with its own goals, conduct and welfare for the benefit of all who participate in it, sport as an institution, which is typically a large-scale bureaucratic organization, is as much if not more concerned with its regulation and administration as well as its promotion as a commodity to be publicized, packaged and sold to those who wish to make use of it for one reason or another. Whereas sport as a valued human practice is or should be universal in its demands and expectations, sport as an institution is almost invariably subject to the particular political and socio-economic demands and pressures that are a part of its particular context. In arguing that sport both is and should be a universally understood and an inherently moral enterprise I shall be mainly concerned with it as a practice rather than as an institution. It is perhaps worth noting, however, that when philosophers conceptually analyse sport they tend to do so in terms of it being a practice and when anthropologists and/or sociologists empirically study sport they tend to think of it in terms of it being an institution within a particular culture or society.

In the light of what has been said it will not be surprising to learn that for some sociologists, sport is seen as but a mirror or microcosm of society, and as such reflects the values (and maladies) of the particular society of which it is a part. Eitzen and Sage (1989, p. 634), for example, write: 'sport must be understood as a set of social practices and relations structured by the culture in which it exists'. Sport when looked upon in this way is a form of relativism. It is maintained that sport can only be seen and understood in terms of its context and that sport in London is not the same as it is in Lagos. This is so, it is argued, because cultural differences, whether they be social, religious, political or economic, impact upon sport and make it different. In so far as this can be shown to be true, it is an accurate thesis in that it is based upon a description of what is the case. It may therefore be regarded as a form of cultural relativism, which recognizes that there are differences in the way life is lived between one part of the world and another.[3] The question that arises, however, is whether or not sport should be seen and understood only in these terms. The answer to this is surely 'no', especially if this implies that there can be legitimate differences about the way in which the rules are interpreted or about how sport should be conducted in general.

In principle at least the practice of sport cuts across national and cultural differences and, like an ideology, provides a set of beliefs and values which are both idealistic and prescriptive. Put differently, is not sport most clearly understood when seen as a valued human practice that transcends cultural differences rather than merely reflecting them? Certainly, from the conceptual point of view, it would seem that sport, and the rules, traditions and values it embodies and which are officially recognized by such bodies as the International Olympic Committee and the World Sporting Federations, are universal in nature and not relative. In the Olympic Charter (*International Olympic Committee*, 1994, pp. 10–11), for example, it is made clear that sport requires mutual understanding based on universal ethical principles and conduct in a spirit of friendship, solidarity and fair play. Tennis, whether played in Boston or Bombay, is not only subject to the same rules of its international governing body but to the same concepts and skills. The terms 'serve', 'ace', 'volley', 'dropshot' and 'lob', and the way they are employed in relation to a particular tactic or strategy, are part of what is now a common stock of knowledge. Wimbledon is a global event in the calendar of tennis and is followed and understood by people of diverse cultures throughout the world. In an attempt to bring increased commonality to the manner in which sport is practised, it is now the case with international federations that their officials meet regularly not only about how best to interpret the rules but how best to apply them in a consistent way for all contestants no matter where the action takes place. It will be seen that sport as a practice is premised upon the rules being the same for all regardless of context or culture. In this way it aspires to be universalistic rather than relativistic.

It is not without interest that Lasch (1979, p. 204), a sociologist, commenting on American society some twenty years ago, observed that: 'The mirror theory of sport, like all reductionist theories of culture, makes no allowance for the autonomy of cultural traditions.' The insightful nature of this statement could now perhaps be more accurately rephrased to read 'trans-cultural traditions'. Certainly it is the hope of Olympism that as and when the young people of the world are properly inducted into sport as a worthwhile practice and find satisfaction in it, they will become more committed to its values and in consequence will become less prone to the influences that adversely affect it.

Although, then, it is possible to recognize that environmental and socio-economic circumstances differ from one culture or society to another or even from one school to another in the same country, it does not follow from this that how sport as a practice should be understood and how it should be conducted must also differ. This same point applies to such specific variables within particular cultures or societies such as race, colour, gender, social class and so on. What should be understood about the practice of sport is that its ethical basis is no less universal than its distinctive concepts and skills. What should be noted in particular is that cultural relativism does not necessarily entail ethical relativism. A related point here, as Thiroux (1990, p. 81) points out, is that 'there is no necessary connection between what *is* or what people *do*, and what *should* be or what they *ought* to do'. What then I want to emphasize here and come back to later, is that when a person enters the practice of sport he or she becomes obligated to its inherent moral demands no less than he or she becomes committed to an understanding and practice of its characteristic concepts and physical skills.

It was suggested earlier that the idea of sport as a reflection of society tends to be a sociological one, but not all sociologists, as has been indicated, accept this one-way and somewhat reductionist view of sport in relation to society and its values. Coakley (1986, p. 35), for example, recognizes that institutions in society can change society rather than just reflect it. Morgan (1994, p. 1), a critical theorist, supports this view. He writes: 'I am convinced that the critical rehabilitation of sport is crucial to the critical rehabilitation of society itself.' Even though this conviction may seem overly optimistic it should not be overlooked that sport as an institution in society is capable of influencing society no less than being influenced by it. If sport, however, is to do this for the betterment of society it is best left to pursue its own values, standards and excellences and not by attempting to act upon society with explicit missionary zeal. If this can be accepted it follows that sport needs to be clear about its own values as a practice. One way of helping to clarify what this involves is to look at the difference between instrumental and intrinsic values.

Briefly, it can be said that instrumental values are those tools, goods, services or activities that can usefully and effectively be employed in the realization of something else that is desired, be it a product, purpose or state of mind. Thus, for example, it can be said of a knife that it is good for peeling potatoes, of exercise that it is a means of improving bodily fitness, of religion that it provides hope, or of the law that it gives justice. Intrinsic values, on the other hand, are perhaps best understood as goods or activities that are desirable or valued in themselves. They are often referred to as ends to which other things are the means. Pleasure, for example, is an end which can be achieved in a variety of ways. A game like chess can be regarded as an intrinsically rewarding activity because of the internally generated puzzles and enjoyment it offers. The same is true of an activity like mathematics. It is in itself of interest regardless of the use to which it can be put. It is the source of its own distinctive purposes, achievements and satisfactions.

Whereas the means people adopt to bring about ends are often matters of fact and can in principle be empirically investigated, the question of what ends are the most valuable is one about which there has been a great deal of philosophic debate.

How then, does what has been said about values relate to sport? It lies, I suggest, in the way sport is thought about and entered into. It can be seen as a means or as an end. When sport is seen as a means it tends to be regarded as but a vehicle in the furtherance of goals and purposes that are external to its intrinsic makeup and demands. When this happens in a particular culture or society it tends to be used for the purposes and values of that society and thereby reflects it. When, on the other hand, sport is seen as a desirable end and is valued for itself in the form of its own skills, excellences, ethical principles and moral virtues, it will be pursued for what they are and thereby remain free of the external cultural or societal influences and pressures with which it comes into contact. When sport is seen in this way, no matter where it is played, it can be said to have universal rather than relative worth.

It will be seen that the notion of sport as a 'reflection' of society is something of a chameleon. On the one hand it gives credence to the view that sport both endorses and embodies the ideals a society may have of itself. On the other hand it recognizes that sport is open and vulnerable to those influences and pressures in society that are questionable and can sometimes be even undermining and corruptive. In American society, for example, sport is often projected in the media as encapsulating and promoting such values as democracy, freedom, equality, individualism, achievement, character development and patriotism but at the same time the vested interests of big business, entertainment, religion and politics help to legitimate the view that sport is little more than a means to bring about worldly success in terms of profit, status, prestige, or power. The most dominant sports creed, according to Edwards (1973, p. 334), is that of 'individual achievement through competition'.

It is a matter of interest that some recent observers of sport in relation to society such as Lasch (1979), Gibson (1993) and Morgan (1994), lament the impact that such extraneous forces can and do have on the practice of sport. Their collective message is that when the intrinsic values of sport are replaced by those that are external to it, there is the distinct possibility that it will be manipulated or worse irredeemably undermined and corrupted. If this diagnosis can be taken as a reasonably correct one, what can be done about it? I suggest at least two things: first, that sport should conceptually free itself as far as possible from its relativistic and instrumental connotations and spell out more clearly what its own intrinsic values are; and second, that once this has been done, more attention should be paid to a more informed and effective pedagogy of sport in schools, colleges and other institutions as a form of education. Only when this has been accomplished is sport likely to be in a position of becoming not only a formative influence in the growth of an individual but in all communities and cultures throughout the world. It can then take its place, not unlike science, as a distinctive and universal form of life.

In looking next at the first of these points it should be made clear that we are concerned here only with the intrinsic moral values of sport.

MORAL VALUES AND THE PRACTICE OF SPORT

The concept and practice of sport, it has been suggested, is intrinsically concerned with moral values. This is not to say that sport is concerned only with moral values (some sports are concerned also with, for example, aesthetic values), but rather that ethical principles and moral conduct form an inherent and crucial part of what should be practised. What I want to argue more particularly is that moral values in sport are universal and prescriptive in nature rather than relative. Whereas ethical relativism maintains that what is right is relative to different cultures, moral values, including those in sport, are characterized by having universal principles that are applicable to all persons regardless of their cultural setting.[4] In short, sport is a form of moral objectivism which holds that certain types of value and conduct such as fairness have universal validity. All who participate in it are expected to comply with what is morally demanded. It is partially because of this that sport should not be seen as a form of 'cultural imperialism', foisted by the West upon the rest of the world, as it is sometimes suggested, with all the unsavoury connotations of imposition that this invokes, but rather as a valued practice that has been freely adopted by different nations and cultures as something that unites, challenges and enriches the manner in which life can be lived.

To engage in sport is to become a member of a worldwide practice community. Each member has not only rights but obligations and is expected to be committed to and live out the values, including moral ones, that are intrinsic to the practice. Looked at then from the moral point of view, sport is not relative but is instead a form of moral universalism. The values it both instantiates and expects are or should be the same for everybody. It will be seen then, that the cultural setting in which sport takes place may vary but the ethical principles and values that underpin and characterize it do not. To make this conceptual point, however, is not to claim that what is expected is invariably practised. Clearly, this is not the case. What is required, however, is not to look for explanations (or excuses) in terms of cultural differences but a greater endeavour and consistency about the way in which the young, no matter where they live, are taught and inducted into sport as a moral practice. What I wish to question and refute then, is the claim by some anthropologists and sociologists that the values of sport are necessarily and inevitably culturally determined. If this were the case the idea of sport as a universal practice would be doomed. In my view, this is not the case and need not be so. The coming together of the world in and through sport is a promising one and with the aid of a common and well-prepared initiation, particularly perhaps in the context of education, can yet be accomplished. This should become an explicit aim of Olympism.[5]

What then more specifically are the moral bases upon which sport both is and should be founded? In common with the idea of an objective morality in general, a morality of sport should be concerned with the adoption of such principles as universality and impartiality and the rules that arise from them should apply to everybody without qualification or exception in the interests of what is fair. Such principles should also provide guidelines for practical use and help in adjudicating between what is 'right' and 'wrong' in a given situation. The rules formulated should be rational and objective so that they can be changed if necessary following open discussion and public agreement. Being morally autonomous in sport implies that a person is able to regulate his or her conduct in terms of the practice and its rules that are freely adopted. Morality in sport, as elsewhere, requires that a person is aware of his or her situation and is responsible for what is done or is not done. All in all, the morally educated contestant will understand that morality in sport is not only to do with obeying the rules of a particular activity but in part lies in his or her own attitude and disposition towards them. It is sometimes said of moral rules that it is not enough to follow them, but it is also necessary to believe in them and to live them out willingly in terms of the actions taken.

It should be understood, however, that whilst rules based upon such principles as universality and impartiality provide a framework for moral action in sport, they by no means exhaust it. As Solomon (1984, p. 15) observes, 'emphasis on principles is not the whole of ethics'. Character and virtue also matter. Such virtues as courage, honesty and compassion have a place in the morality of sport no less than a willing observance of the rules. Moral life in sport would be impoverished without their presence. They are particularly important to a practice like sport for without them it would never become all that it can be and should be. Virtues such as fairness, friendliness and magnanimity, according to MacIntyre (1985, p. 191), are not only cardinal features of a practice but are necessary to the realization of its intrinsic purposes and values. Furthermore, they help safeguard it from being corrupted by such external considerations as power, status, prestige and money.

What I am arguing then is that sport as a universal valued practice is best understood and characterized in terms of the principles, rules and virtues that both underlie and constitute it. The Kantian and Aristotelian traditions in moral theory,[6] it seems to me, provide the most apposite perspectives for this understanding. The former provides a reasoned account of how such fundamental principles as universality and impartiality relate to such considerations as duty, obligation and fairness. The latter provides an account of the development of the individual who, in order to achieve fulfilment as a person, requires that certain virtues, such as courage, honesty and justice, are cultivated and practised, not only in relation to the individual's own well-being but also in relation to the larger community – the trans-cultural community. It will be seen, for example, that acts of sportspersonship, although not demanded by the rules, are an embodiment of its best traditions. Acts that are motivated by such virtues as generosity, magnanimity and a concern for others, are not only admired as attributes of what it is to be a person but help characterize the nature and ethos of sport as a practice.

What then 'good' sport both exemplifies and requires, from the moral point of view, is not only a willing adherence to the rules based upon an informed understanding of them but also other forms of conduct that are not required by the rules but which are nonetheless recognized as being in keeping with its highest traditions. Whereas the Kantian tradition emphasizes fairness, duty and obligation, the Aristotelian tradition emphasizes the exercise and display of appropriate virtues that are often over and beyond what the rules lay down, but which nevertheless are conducive to its ethos as a valued practice.

SPORT AND EDUCATION

What, it may be asked, in the light of what has been said, is the relationship between sport and education? The answer to this question, of course, depends upon what is meant by education. As in the case of other aspects of life it is useful to distinguish between the factual and the evaluative. A descriptive account of education is an attempt to report on 'how things are' without any judgements of value necessarily being made about whether they are good, bad or indifferent. An evaluative account, on the other hand, is an attempt to appraise and provide considered judgements about 'what ought to be' in terms of content and its relationship to upbringing and learning. Whereas the former is concerned with facts, the latter is concerned with values. An evaluative account of education is inevitably directed to such questions as: 'Which values are the most appropriate or necessary to being educated?' or 'Which activities are of most worth?'.

When confronted with such fundamental questions it is not unusual for philosophers of education to look at such values as happiness, knowledge, moral virtue and self-realization.[7] Theories abound about what is entailed by these values and how they relate to one another.[8] What it is important to realize, however, is that an evaluative account of education is dependent upon a consideration of values and that, whatever is decided about their place and priority, they then in effect prescribe what is to happen.

The evaluative account of education in relation to which I shall consider sport, is that of the initiation view. Originally it was formulated by Hirst and Peters (1970) but because of its intellectual bias I have modified it to include such physical practices as sport and dance.[9] Its value base, however, I have retained. Briefly, the initiation view of education is one that involves the young being initiated into those worthwhile aspects of human endeavour that are available to them. In the West, for example, such subjects as science, technology, mathematics, language, history and the arts would normally be expected to find a place in the curriculum. For Peters (1966a, pp. 144–66), what marks out an activity or subject as being worthwhile is that it features knowledge and understanding. More than this, it requires that *how* something is taught is no less important than *what* is taught. What this last point emphasizes is that the procedures or methods adopted must be moral ones.[10] A further point is that the activities taught, whether 'theoretical' or 'practical', should be pursued for their own sake rather than for a purpose that is external to them. Whereas 'education' is best understood as an initiation into a culture's worthwhile practices in a morally defensible way for their own intrinsic worth, 'schooling' by contrast is more concerned with the pursuit of subjects as a means to something else.[11] Thus, education is concerned with the pursuit of its own ends and not those that lie outside of itself. It is of intrinsic worth and not only of instrumental value. It is concerned as much with attitude and interest as it is with subject matter. What should be made clear is that because an activity has intrinsic worth it is not precluded also from having instrumental value. Painting, for example, can be pursued for its own merits as well as for its therapeutic value. The role of the teacher *qua* educationist, however, is not to be a therapist, even though unwittingly therapeutic effects may result. Rather it is to initiate the pupil into the understanding and practice of painting. Educational 'objectives', it will be seen, should not be confused with incidental or fortuitous 'outcomes'.

Perhaps enough has been said to show that the view of sport as a valued human practice and the initiation view of education are very much in accord with one another. They are in fact compatible. Indeed, it can be said that when sport is pursued for its own internal goals in the form of its skills, tactics, strategies and standards in a moral way for their own sake, it is in and of itself educative. The practical knowledge of which it is made up and the moral qualities which it both demands and is dependent upon make it worthwhile. When lived out they constitute what it is to be in an educative situation.

In contradistinction to what has been said above, however, it will be appreciated that sport, even within the institution of the school, can be used for political, social or economic ends. Huxley (1969, pp. 187–8), for example, well understood this. He observes:

> Like every other instrument that man has invented, sport can be used for good or evil purposes. Used well, it can teach endurance and encourages a sense of fair play and a respect for rules, coordinated effort and subordination of personal interests to those of

the group. Used badly it can encourage personal vanity and group vanity, greedy desire for victory and hatred for rivals, an intolerant *esprit de corps* and contempt for people who are beyond a certain selected pale.

In the light of what has been said about education in its evaluative sense, however, the question that arises is should sport be used at all? The answer to this is that it should not be. Rather it should remain true to itself. It should be engaged in for the values, standards and excellences that characterize it, not for purposes, good or bad, that lie outside it. Both Dewey (1916, pp. 89–90) and Peters (1966a, pp. 144–66) are insistent that the content and the procedures adopted for the teaching of subjects should be intrinsically valuable. Interestingly, it is not only philosophers who recognize the pedagogic point implicit here, but also some sociologists. Lasch (1979, p. 182), for example, observes that: 'Games quickly lose their charm when forced into the service of education, character development or social improvement.'

What emerges from this brief discussion about values in relation to sport and education is that if sport is to secure a firm place in the curriculum and be justified in educational terms, rather than in terms of schooling (i.e. being seen only as a means in the promotion of such extrinsic purposes as health, socialization or therapy), it should be perceived as a valued human practice and pursued because in and of itself it is found to be worthwhile. Such 'purposes' as the ones mentioned, which are often given as reasons as to why sport should be taught in schools, should be regarded, if and when they occur, as its beneficial outcomes rather than as its objectives. It is only by getting pupils to engage in and appreciate the intrinsic values of sport, including its skills, traditions, achievements and moral virtues, that its distinctive worthwhile ness can be upheld, thus justifying its teaching in schools and colleges as a part of the educational curriculum.

SUMMARY

In summary I have argued three things. First, that sport as a valued human practice is best understood in terms of universalism rather than in terms of relativism. This implies that what is involved both conceptually and morally is applicable to all peoples in the world, despite the fact that they come from different cultures and will have different thoughts and beliefs about a variety of other things. Second, that this approach to sport entails looking at it from the point of view of its intrinsic values rather than from the point of view of its possible instrumental ones. A correlative outcome of this approach, especially with regard to the employment of the virtues, is that it is likely to help save sport as an institution from being unduly and adversely affected by potential (and actual) external corruptive forces. Third, that sport can only be considered as being compatible with education, rather than as just a useful means, providing its own internal values in the form of skills, standards and excellences are considered worthwhile and pursued in a moral manner for their own sake.

It is to a further exploration of the moral dimensions of sport as a valued human practice and the implications of this for the conduct of sport and the place of sport in education that the next few chapters are devoted.

NOTES

1. See The Miller Lite Report (1983).
2. For further discussion on the relationship between practices and institutions, internal and external goals as well as the function of virtues in relation to sport, see McNamee (1995).
3. Relativism denies that there are certain kinds of universal truths. It is normally recognized that there are two main types, cognitive and ethical. *Cognitive relativism* holds that there are no universal truths about the world; there are just different ways of interpreting it. *Ethical relativism* maintains that what is considered morally 'right' and 'wrong' varies from society to society and that there are no moral principles accepted by all societies. Critics of cognitive relativism contend that when relativists present statements as being universally, rather than relatively, true they become logically incoherent. It should be noted that the opposite of ethical relativism is *ethical objectivism*, which asserts that although some cultures or societies may differ in their moral behaviour, some moral principles have universal validity.

    For further explication of these terms, see the article on relativism by Pojman in Audi (1995, pp. 690–1).
4. In many ways morality in sport is not unlike the human rights movement which is based upon the belief that everybody should have certain inalienable rights accorded them (e.g. the right not to be tortured) by virtue of being human and that such rights as those formulated by the United Nations (1948) should be respected. For a useful summary of the major documents concerning the International Human Rights movement see Winston (1989). For a book devoted to the ethics behind the idea of human rights, see Nino (1993), also Melden (1980).
5. It is only by being true to itself that sport is more likely to fulfil the mission created for it by the spirit of Olympism. That is, to educate and cultivate the individual in and through sport, to cultivate good relationships between all peoples of the world, to promote international understanding and to celebrate human greatness and possibility. See Loland (1995) and Arnold (1996).
6. For a clear introduction to each of these positions, see Sullivan (1994) and Urmson (1988).
7. Useful books to consult here are those by Singer (1994) and Hospers (1990).
8. A helpful summary of educational theories is provided by Bigge (1982). See also Frankena (1965).
9. For an elaboration of this point, see Arnold (1988).

    It is of interest to note on this point that in recent years Hirst (1993, pp. 184–99) has altered his view of what education is or should be. Instead of it being essentially academic in nature and primarily concerned with an induction into the theoretically based forms of knowledge and understanding, he now believes as I do that education is best conceived, at least in its basic sense, as an initiation into a culture's worthwhile practices with all that this implies with regard to the values, skills, standards and virtues that both characterize and sustain them. Instead of being concerned with the development of 'mind', he now speaks of the development of 'persons' that takes account of their full range of feelings, dispositions and capacities.
10. One reason for the neglect of sport as a moral practice, I suspect, at least in the literature, is that sport has been seen by some philosophers of education as a form of play which is thought of as being discontinuous with the 'serious' business of life and therefore of no moral importance. Dearden (1968, p. 100), for example, writes of play (and by implication sport) when he refers to it as being 'non-serious' in the sense of it being apart from the duties, deliberations and developing projects which make up the web of purposes of everyday life. Peters (1966a, p. 159) too, writes: 'part of what is meant by calling something a game [he has in mind here games like cricket] is that it is set apart from the main business of living, complete in itself, and limited to particular times and places'. Both philosophers, it is of interest to note, seem to have been influenced by Huizinga (1970,

p. 320) who first gave credence to the view that play, including sport, is separate from real life when he spoke of it as being a 'free activity standing, quite consciously, outside "ordinary life" and "non serious"'.

11.   For a further elaboration of the distinction between education and schooling as well as the intrinsic and extrinsic values of sport, see Arnold (1991).

Chapter 2

Sport as a Valued Human Practice: A Basis for the Consideration of Some Moral Issues in Sport

In Chapter 1 it was argued that sport has now reached the point in its evolution and development in the world that it is best considered as a universally valued practice with inherent moral concerns and that when it is viewed and taught in this way it becomes a justifiable part of the educational curriculum in schools, colleges and other places of learning that are concerned with its welfare. The task now is to explicate further what is meant by sport as a practice and show more explicitly how this differs from sport as an institution.

Before embarking on this it is worth noting that over the past few years interest in the ethical aspects of sport has increased considerably. Despite the growing number of publications in this area, however, few have been concerned with the ethical basis of sport itself.[1] It is because I believe an account of sport as a valued human practice can provide normative criteria by means of which it is possible to assist with the making of moral judgements in and about sport that I propose to give such an account here.

What I wish to submit in brief is that it is not yet sufficiently recognized that sport, like science or medicine, is a particular type of human practice that has its own integrity and is governed and characterized by its rules and ethos. Such practices are, of course, open to abuse but essentially they are distinctive forms of worthwhile life. Together they not only constitute what it is to be in a culture but are the source of our possibilities and values as civilized persons. It is only when sport is understood in this way that moral issues in relation to sport become fully intelligible.

SPORT AS A CULTURALLY VALUED HUMAN PRACTICE

Sport is by no means a simple term. Along with the terms 'play' and 'game' it forms a part of what has been referred to as the 'tricky triad'.[2] In much of the literature these terms are used almost interchangeably. Over the years this has caused considerable confusion. More recently, attempts have been made to use such terms in a more discriminating manner. It is now commonly, if not universally, agreed that whereas 'play' refers to an activity that is pursued voluntarily for its own sake, the term 'game' is best characterized as a rule-bound goal-directed activity in which the rules agreed upon limit the permissible means of goal attainment. In play the attitude and effort of the player is directed towards the intrinsic reward of the activity. Although many games are directed towards their intrinsic rewards they are best characterized by the type of rules that govern them, whether they be the card game of bridge or the game of cricket. What marks out sport, apart from its goal-directed and rule-bound features, is that additionally it is concerned with physical skill and prowess. It should be noted that although play can enter into both games and sport, sport is distinctive in that it places a premium on bodily skill and frequently upon strength, speed and stamina as, for example, in track and field or in the playing of football or rugby.[3]

What should be made clear is that I am concerned here only with what might be called person-to-person sports which are commonly taught in schools and other educational institutions, and not with that whole range of pastimes including such activities as hunting, shooting and fishing which are sometimes categorized as sports.

Although the central features of play, games and sport, as briefly described above, tell us something of their inter-relationships and differences, they tell us little about the nature of sport as a culturally valued human practice that has a long history and is now a worldwide phenomenon.

Sport, of course, had its origins in a variety of ancient cultures, but its modern form stems predominantly from Europe and especially perhaps from ancient Greece and nineteenth century England. It was in the public schools of Britain during the time of the industrial revolution that team games particularly were encouraged not so much on grounds of physical development and health but rather because it was believed they fostered such virtues as leadership, respect, loyalty, courage, honesty, fair play, sportsmanship, self-reliance and self-discipline. Group solidarity, team spirit and pride in one's school were qualities that were also promoted and emphasized. The ethos that was encapsulated in and through sport was that of the Christian gentleman. Modern sport owes a lot to the way it was conceived and codified in the nineteenth century movement in Britain known as 'muscular Christianity'.[4] Although each sport has a unique pattern of evolution, the rules that govern and characterize them are based upon the social principles of justice and equality. The distinction that is often made between the constitutive rules (or game-defining rules) and regulative rules (or penalty-invoking rules) is a formal way of attempting to preserve the social and ethical basis upon which sport was founded. Certainly, for example, within the English public school tradition, the notion of sport without sportsmanship would have been inconceivable.

The fundamental principles[5] of the Olympic movement also uphold that competition shall be fair and equal and state that there shall be no discrimination on grounds of race, religion, politics or sex (p. 13). The Olympic ideal, among other things, aims to promote and strengthen friendship between sportsmen of all countries.[6] For Baron de Coubertin, who is regarded as being responsible for the re-establishment of the Olympic Games in modern times and who was profoundly influenced by the pedagogical doctrines of Thomas Arnold (1795–1842), Headmaster of Rugby School, sport was not only regarded as an aspect of physical culture, based upon the spirit of chivalry, but also as a form of aesthetic education.[7] In the *Olympic Charter*

(International Olympic Committee, 1994, p. 10) one of the fundamental principles of Olympism is stated as being 'to place sport at the service of the harmonious development of man, with a view to encouraging the establishment of a peaceful society concerned with the preservation of human dignity'. Another refers to a way of life that is based upon a respect for universal ethical principles (p. 10).

The point about these somewhat brief remarks is to suggest that sport, despite its more recent perverted and unsavoury connections, is a culturally valued practice that embodies some of the highest human ideals and most cherished traditions. When a sport is pursued for its own sake, its rules willingly followed and its finest conventions upheld, sport becomes an ennobling and worthwhile form of life. It is the sort of human practice by which individuals can be judged and civilization tested. When, on the other hand, a sport is used by individuals, institutions or society only for the values or goals that are associated with it, be they political or commercial, there is a danger that it will become but a means to these ends and so have its nature as an inherently worthwhile human practice altered and corrupted. It is, therefore, important to understand more specifically what is meant by the term 'practice' and in what senses it is culturally valuable.

Following MacIntyre (1985, p. 187) I shall adopt the word 'practice' to mean:

> Any coherent and complex form of socially established co-operative human activity through which goods internal to that form of activity are realised in the course of trying to achieve those standards of excellence which are appropriate to, and partially definitive of, that form of activity, with the result that human powers to achieve excellence, and human conceptions of the ends and goods involved are systematically extended.[8]

Like farming, physics, engineering or architecture, sport is a practice because it is a peculiarly human activity in which values internal to that activity are discovered and realized in the course of trying to achieve the standards of excellence that characterize it. As MacIntyre (1985, p. 190) puts it:

> A practice involves standards of excellence and obedience to rules as well as the achievement of goods. To enter into a practice is to accept the authority of those standards and the inadequacy of my own performance as judged by them. It is to subject my own attitudes, choices, preferences and tastes to the standards which currently and partially define the practice.

As has been shown in the case of sport, a practice has a history and has evolved over a period of time. Thus, the standards are not fixed or immune from criticism and change. When a person is initiated into a practice it will be done in such a way that he or she will be expected to accept the authority of the best standards of that practice realized so far, whether it be in the field of baseball or ballet, music or mathematics. If, on starting to learn tennis, I do not accept that others, well versed in tennis, know better than I how to serve and when to volley, there is little chance of developing such skills or appreciations. In sporting, as with other practices, the standards that apply are those that are objective, not subjective or emotional, and relate to its intrinsic goals and purposes rather than to those that are extrinsic. Furthermore, every practice, if it is to remain true to itself and not be corrupted by influences or pressures external to it, requires a certain kind of relationship between those who participate in it, whether they like one another or not, or whether, as in many instances of sport, they find themselves opposed to one another in competition.

Unless the participants in a practice see one another with respect and as being common guardians of the values inherent in the practice they are pursuing, the practice itself is likely to suffer and perhaps fall victim to the unprincipled and the unscrupulous. In order to preserve the integrity of practices, so that participants in them uphold and pursue the internal goods and standards of excellence that characterize them, it is necessary that such qualities as justice, honesty and courage are fostered and encouraged. Such virtues, as MacIntyre (1985, p. 191) calls them, are not only necessary components of practices but also help identify them.

Justice requires that everybody in the practice is treated fairly and in accord with objective or impersonal standards of achievement or conduct. Honesty requires that truthfulness is observed so that trust can be generated between one practitioner and another. Courage requires the capacity to risk harm or danger to oneself out of care and concern for the goals, values and standards of the practice. One of the central features of practices then, is that they both need such virtues as the ones mentioned, and provide opportunities for them to be cultivated and developed. This remains true of a practice like sport, regardless of whether its practitioners differ in political outlook, religious belief or live in different parts of the world. What makes such virtues indispensable to a practice is that without them it would be impossible to pursue satisfactorily the values and excellences that help constitute and characterize it. What is being said here is that when a person enters into sport as a practice he or she becomes a member of an extended community, a community which is distinguished by its fraternal bonds and commitments. Each and every member is expected to devote himself or herself to the internal goals and values that together they share and for which they are jointly and severally responsible. It is this sense of being in a community that is important to all practices. It not only provides a framework for the nurturing and cultivation of such social virtues as sympathy, compassion and generosity but also an opportunity to develop a feeling of group identity.

Blum (1994, p. 146), in discussing the relationship between virtue and community in the writings of MacIntyre, identifies a number of propositions which, if true, are of central importance not only to the teaching of sport but to education in general. The first is that virtues can only be learned within a particular form of social life. The second is that virtues once developed can only be sustained in communities. On this point MacIntyre (1984, p. 10), observes that: 'I need those around me to reinforce my moral strengths, and assist me in rectifying my moral weaknesses. It is in general only within a community that individuals become capable of morality, and are sustained in their morality.' The third is that it is only by living in a form of social life (or participating in a particular practice) that one can learn the relevant situation-descriptions, the forms of perception and consciousness and habits of action, that give content to our understanding and conduct. What should be added, in the light of what is to be said later, is that the ethics of virtue (or what some people call communitarianism) should not be seen as an alternative to the ethics of impartiality and universality, but rather as a complement to it. This, I think, is particularly true of sport when seen as a valued human practice.

It will be seen that the practice-community of sport is not unlike that of the practice-community of scholarship. The scholar, as a member of a community devoted to the pursuit of truth, will be expected to work in accord with what this demands with reference to his particular discipline. Good scholarship can be characterized by such virtues as being thorough (looking at all the available evidence, considering alternative hypotheses and interpretations, etc.), being thoughtful and organized (having a coherent thesis to offer and not just a collection of facts and figures), being honest (acknowledging sources and presenting the evidence as it is found and not manipulating it to suit a particular thesis or viewpoint), being clear (so that what is said can be understood by others) and being open-minded and tolerant of the valid criticism of others. It is when such virtues as these are practised that scholarship will be enhanced, and conversely it is when such corresponding vices as being careless or neglectful, being casual or disorganized, being dishonest, being unclear, inconsistent or confusing, being closed-minded and unwilling to accept reasoned criticism are practised, that the idea of scholarship is negated. The analogy being made here is that the practice of sport, like the practice of scholarship, is dependent upon the necessity as well as the exemplification of virtues and the condemnation and absence of vices. Without both sets of conditions operating there is always the danger that a practice will be discredited and die.

It has been argued then that sport as a valued cultural practice is best thought of as having its own internal goals and excellences and that these are upheld and sustained by its participants possessing and employing certain forms of virtue. Indeed, a practice, like a profession, is characterized as much by the moral way its participants conduct themselves as in the skills they develop and the purposes to which they are committed. What makes each practice distinctive, is that its internal goals are so called for two reasons. First, they can only be specified and understood in terms of that particular activity (e.g. squash or croquet). Second, they can only be fully appreciated by those who know the activity in question from the inside. A reverse angle shot in squash, for example, can only be understood in terms of that activity, just as it can only be fully appreciated (how and when to play it, etc.) when one is or has been an initiated participant.

In summary it can be said that sport, as a culturally valued practice, can be thought of as:

> A competitive rule-bound physically demanding activity in which its internal goals and standards are pursued in a moral way for their own sake.

What I have suggested so far is that without a clear idea of what sport as a culturally valued practice is, such as the one so far provided – what one might term pure or good sport – there are no guiding principles or criteria by which 'sport' as it is sometimes practised can be evaluated.

It may be thought at least in principle that the practice view of sport cannot be moral in any universal sense because like some other human practices it is culturally relative.[9] This criticism, however, is ill-founded, as has been shown, first, because the rules of its various instances are based upon universal ethical principles, and second, because it is based upon commonly held virtues which are indigenous to and characteristic of it as a particular kind of practice-community which is now worldwide.

THE SOCIOLOGICAL VIEW OF SPORT IN CONTRAST TO THE PRACTICE VIEW

In general it can be said following MacIntyre (1985, p. 194) that practices are not to be confused with institutions. The game of tennis, for example, is not to be mistaken for the International Tennis Federation. Whereas a practice is concerned with the preservation of its own internal goods, standards of achievement and conduct, institutions, although expressing concern with these same things, are characteristically concerned as much, if not more, with the control and distribution of external goods in the form of power, status, prestige and money. When a practice like sport becomes institutional, its organization and administration become bureaucratized. Officials are expected to fulfil a number of particular functions concerned with such matters as its promotion, sponsorship and ritualization. The institutionalization of sport[10] at both an amateur and professional level, has led to the rules of the practice becoming standardized, rule enforcement being taken over by the appropriate regulatory authority, the organizational and technical aspects of the practice becoming highly developed and the learning of skills becoming formalized and systematized. What makes the institutionalization of sport different from its practice is that whereas the former is concerned with many factors including those concerned with its large-scale organization and its promotion and distribution of external goods, the latter is concerned only with the pursuit and enhancement of its internal goods. It is these in themselves that are found to be worthwhile. They may also come to represent new heights of human achievement.

The social analyst, in an attempt to be descriptively objective rather than evalua-tively prescriptive, will quickly come to see that sport reflects both intrinsic and extrinsic considerations. Thus, for example, Coakley (1986, p. 17) defines sport as: 'An institutionalised competitive activity that involves vigorous physical exertion or the use of relatively complex physical skills by individuals whose participation is motivated by a combination of intrinsic and extrinsic factors.' What is to be noticed about the above definition, in contrast to the one previously given of sport as a culturally valued practice, is that there is explicit reference to 'external goals' and that these as much as 'internal goals' can, for the competitors, form the motivational basis of their participation. It no longer implies that sport, to count as sport, be done only in pursuit of its own excellences and standards. Instead it can be done perhaps predominantly for extrinsic reasons. It will be seen then that what I have called the 'practice view' of sport differs noticeably from what I shall call the 'sociological view'. Whereas the practice view is concerned with the identification of sport as a culturally valued practice in which standards and conduct immanent in the practice are vigilantly applied because they are in themselves found to be worthwhile, the sociological view sees sport as an institutionalized social phenomenon in which individuals participate for a variety of reasons, some intrinsic, some extrinsic. The practice view of sport represents a total commitment to the pursuit of the practice's internal goals in a moral way by each participant through the employment of such virtues as honesty, justice and courage. In contrast, the sociological view of sport, although officially applauding such virtues and values, recognizes that in reality participants are often more concerned with the use of sport as an instrument in the pursuit of such external goals as power, prestige, status and money. It is when the pursuit of external goals comes to be seen as more important than those which are internal, that sport as a practice is in danger of being irredeemably perverted and corrupted. It can be said that whereas the practice view is idealistic and prescriptive, the sociological view is realistic and descriptive. It is the difference between sport as it *ought* to be and sport as it *is*. What should be made clear is that practices do not necessarily become corrupted when they become institutionalized – sometimes institutions can be sustaining and supportive – it is only that there is a tendency for them to become so. This tendency is perhaps most in evidence in the case of professional sport, where competition is at a high level and there is a lot at stake, particularly in the form of external goals, especially economic.

Two related factors should be borne in mind about external goods in relation to sport. The first is that such goods, unlike internal goods, can invariably be obtained in other ways. The second is that because of this, their connection with sport is only a contingent one. It will be seen, for example, that an external good like money can be obtained in a variety of ways unrelated to sport but an internal good is logically related to the nature of sport itself. An important corollary to this is that when an external good has been achieved it normally becomes the sole possession of the person (or team) concerned, whereas with the achievement of internal goods in the form of new skills and standards, for example, the whole community associated with that practice, participants and followers alike, derive benefit.

It should be understood then, as some sport theorists like Morgan (1987, pp. 17–18) do understand, that the ethos of sport as a practice can be quite different from the climate that can sometimes pervade the sociological view of sport. These two depictions of sport, as will now be clear, are by no means necessarily at ease with one another. How the practice view relates to the sociological view will vary from one sport to another as well as from one part of the world to another. The commercialization of sport in the United States of America, for example, is probably greater than it is in Uganda. Again, although the ethos of a sport may be influenced to an extent by whether the participants are 'amateur' or 'professional', it is probably not solely determined by such a distinction. In professional golf, for example, despite external goals being available in the form of prestige and money, the ethos of the sport or the moral manner in which it is conducted – what one might call its prevailing spirit, tone or sentiment – is of a noticeably high order. This is often in contrast to such sports as soccer, American football or ice-hockey, where in some parts of the world the 'ethos' of the sport, if it exists at all in any moral sense, is of a low order. This observation is not meant to suggest that the participants in some sports tend to be morally superior to those in others, though this may be the case, but rather that some sports, perhaps because of their nature, are more explicit in the moral and social demands that are entailed by them, than others. Not all sports, for example, refer in their rules to such matters as 'ungentlemanly conduct' or conduct that is 'prejudicial to the good name of the game'.

One other point about the difference between the two views of sport needs to be made clear, and that is to do with the motivation of the participants. It is sometimes maintained[11] that providing the rules are followed, a person's subjective or psychological dispositions are irrelevant to his or her engagement in sport. If the sociological view of sport is to be accepted as the only case of what constitutes sport, this might well be so since motivation can be concerned with either internal or external goals.

If, however, the practice view of sport is accepted as what ought to be the case, the question of what motivates participants is crucially important, for only if their interests and concerns are focused predominantly, if not exclusively, on the pursuit of internal goals and the moral manner in which they are pursued, will the integrity of the practice be preserved. It will be seen then that it is precisely at the point when the external goals of a sport are found to be compellingly attractive that the virtues most associated with sport as a practice are in most need of being exercised.

What seems clear, as some recent critiques of sport have shown,[12] is that the more the practice view of sport is used and abused by the pursuit of external goals and interests, the more perverted and corrupted it is likely to become. Instead of being personally ennobling and socially enriching there is danger of it becoming a vehicle of degradation and alienation. Put differently institutions are likely to corrupt practices when they demonstrate an undue interest in the promotion and extension of external goods at the expense of the preservation and cultivation of internal ones. What is needed in the case of sport management in society is the working out of an acceptable relationship between the twin concerns of internal and external goods. At school level, if the organization of sport is left predominantly in the hands of educators, the conflict of interests, if it exists at all, should not be difficult to resolve.[13] At senior, and particularly professional level, the matter is less easy to deal with and control. One way, however, of reducing the almost inevitable domination and corruption of practices by institutions has been put forward by Morgan (1994). He suggests the setting up of 'practice-communities' (p. 236) as deliberative bodies comprised of primary and secondary agents. Primary agents would come from those who actively pursue a particular activity; secondary agents would come from those who are interested in and concerned about the integrity of sport and have some connection with it, in the form of being coaches, officials, spectators, journalists, scholars, researchers and critics. It would be the prime task of each practice-community to preserve and sustain a fidelity towards the internal goods of each practice so that they were not undermined or compromised by institutions. They would try to reach a rational consensus about contending norms and values and how sport should be operated and controlled. The motivating force behind the practice-community idea is that decisions made would arise from the internal logic of the activity in question and the manner in which it should be conducted rather than the way in which it can act as an instrument in the bringing about of monetary or other external goods. Regrettably Morgan does not go into any detail about whether or not practice-communities are to replace institutions or somehow act in conjunction with them in an effort to try and offset their overpowering influence. Either way the sentiment is clear, and that is that if sport as a practice and as a valuable form of life is to be preserved it must be constantly and vigilantly on guard against the potential and actual corruptive power of the institutions that at present control it.

Overall what has been argued is that a proper understanding of sport as a valued practice involves more than a formal analysis of its meaning in relation to other overlapping terms. It involves also an understanding of its history, traditions and moral implications. The practice view of sport, unlike the sociological view of sport, although governed by the same constitutional rules, is committed to the preservation of its own goals, standards and excellences, rather than to the achievement of externally motivated rewards. It is evaluative and prescriptive in nature and not merely descriptive or factual about a certain form of institutionalized social life. It is important because it provides an ethical basis or framework for the discussion of moral issues in sport without which such issues get buried in a quagmire of ambivalence and uncertainty. What needs to be understood is that in 'good' sport there is a kind of symbiotic relationship between its internal goals and the virtues that render them possible. As MacIntyre (1985, p. 223), in speaking of practices in general, expresses it:

> The virtues find their point and purpose not only in sustaining those relationships necessary if the variety of goals internal to practices are to be achieved and not only in sustaining the form of an individual life in which that individual may seek out his or her goal as the goal of his or her whole life, but also in sustaining those traditions which promote both practices and individual lives with their own historical context.

It has been argued that sport as a culturally valued practice is dependent not only upon its participants pursuing its own goals for their own sake but also on them doing so in a moral way in terms of its rules, conventions and admired traditions. Sport, like other human practices such as science, medicine or the law, requires the exercise of the virtues within something like a community framework if it is to preserve and safeguard its own integrity and its own moral ethos as a distinctive and valuable form of life. This theme is explored in some detail in the next few chapters.

NOTES

1. See, for example, Arnold (1992, 1994), Aspin (1975), Feezell (1988), Fraleigh (1984), Gibson (1993) and Morgan (1994), which are unusual in this respect. See also, however, Hyland (1990), Kretchmar (1994), McIntosh (1979), Meakin (1986), Morgan and Meier (1988), Osterhoudt (1973, 1990), Simon (1991), Thomas (1983) and Vanderwerken and Wertz (1985).
2. This indicative phrase was introduced by Suits (1988) in his debate with Meier (1988) about the relationship between these three terms.
3. For a penetrating analysis of the relationships between play and culture, see Huizinga (1970).
4. Mangan (1981) has written informatively on this topic.
5. See the Olympic Rules and Regulations (1974).
6. See International Olympic Committee, Article 11, (1974).
7. Quoted in Grayham and Ueberhorst (1976, p. 115).
8. What should be made clear here is that although I have adopted MacIntyre's characterization of what a practice is, and how the virtues not only help identify it but are necessary to its flourishing, I do not wish as a result of this to be committed to, or associated with, his overall condemnation of modern liberalism as a solution to contemporary moral problems. Indeed, in Chapter 8, I argue that a liberal education should comprise an initiation of pupils into a range of worthwhile practices such as science or sport, especially when they are pursued for the internal goods they contain. Suffice to say here that I do not see the idea of a liberal education and the idea of a valued human practice as incompatible.
9. As has been explained, cultural relativism is a descriptive thesis and is based upon anthropological observations about what is different between one culture and another. It should be noted, furthermore, that cultural relativism does not necessarily entail ethical relativism, i.e. what is right or wrong is relative or peculiar to a particular culture. It will be seen, for example, that although some cultures will differ in certain respects, they may also be similar in other respects such as in religion or holding particular moral values concerning such matters as incest, lying, cheating and stealing.

It is my contention that sport, as an inter-cultural and trans-cultural social practice, based upon accepted ethical principles, internationally agreed rules and common conventions, is no longer, if ever it was, a culturally relative one but a universal and morally normative one. It should be the mission of all who are interested in the promotion of sport pedagogy and such movements as Olympism to initiate the young into sporting practices in such a way that they both understand and appreciate the values and virtues as well as skills and standards entailed.

As a footnote to the above points it can be said that MacIntyre criticizes modern liberalism on the grounds that it has failed in its attempt to provide an answer to moral life by an appeal to rational principles. This is so because it has not understood that the person is not atomistic in conception but is in part social, and therefore needs, as Aristotle and Aquinus recognized, to take into account the background circumstances and context in which the person is. Instead of liberalism, with its pluralistic factions, continuing to provide interminable and indeterminate debates about how to live and what is 'right' and 'wrong', there is a need to return to something like a communitarian ethic which practices, with their demand for an employment of the virtues, in part provide. For further elaboration on these points see MacIntyre (1988, 1990); also Horton and Mendus (1994).

10. For additional information about what is involved in the institutionalization of sport see, for example, Loy (1969), Coakley (1986) and Eitzen and Sage (1989).
11. See Meier (1981).
12. See, for example, Brohm (1978), Lasch (1979), Gibson (1993) and Morgan (1994).
13. See, for example, Arnold (1992, 1994).

Chapter 3

Three Moral Arguments Against Rule Breaking and the Abuse of Sport

The practice view of sport, it has been suggested, is different from the sociological view of sport. In the case of the former, competition tends to be seen in terms of internal goals and morally desirable outcomes and qualities, whereas in the case of the latter, competition tends to be seen more in terms of external goals and morally objectionable or at least questionable forms of attitude and behaviour. What can reasonably be generalized from these findings, is that the ethos of sport as a culturally valued practice is likely to fall short of its own ideals, moral standards, admired traditions and educationally worthwhile possibilities when (i) external goals come to be seen as more important than internal goals and (ii) perhaps as a result of this, an undue emphasis is placed upon winning so that the result of the competition is held to be more important than the immanent process of struggle and challenge.

It is not a part of my present task to bring corroborative empirical evidence to substantiate such tendencies, though I am sure there would be no great difficulty in doing this; rather it is to show at a conceptual level that when competition in sport is too heavily involved with the pursuit of external goals and/or places too much emphasis on winning, the idea of sport as a culturally valued practice is more likely to become corrupted. This is so because when the pursuit of external goals is seen to be more important than the pursuit of internal goals, the former take priority over the latter; that is to say the key characteristics of sport as a practice – the pursuit of its own skills, standards and excellences for their own sake – get usurped. The ends in effect become reduced to means, means in the service of an extrinsic goal. The transformation of the intrinsic goals of sport as a practice into an instrumental means for the achievement of extrinsic goals or purposes, be they political, social or economic, is to corrupt and undermine it. When this happens sport is no longer pursued in terms of itself but in terms of something else. Such undermining and corrupting should not of course, be seen in terms of black or white but is, according to circumstances, a matter of degree. Whether this is mildly pervasive, as it often is in school sport, or blatantly apparent as is frequently the case in professional sport, the upshot is the same. That is the notion of pure sport or sport as a culturally valued practice is perverted and debased.

THE SYNDROME OF WINNING AT ALL COSTS

So much then for the corruptive tendency of external goals. What now of the over-emphasis on winning? I have suggested elsewhere (Arnold, 1989) in relation to competitive sport that, whereas trying to win is a desirable and necessary feature of a good contest, an over-riding desire to win can lead to an intentional breaking of the rules in the form of 'professional' or faked fouls, in order to gain an unfair advantage. Such forms of behaviour not only contravene the spirit of the practice but indicate a willingness to cheat and to hurt others in the interests of victory. What matters to the participant is not how he or she played the game but rather who won or lost. The ultimate degradation of competitive sport comes when there is not just an over-emphasis on winning but when winning comes to be seen as the only criterion of success. 'To win at all costs' exemplifies an attitude of mind and conduct which is the very antithesis of the ethos of sport as a culturally valued practice. It signifies a call for victory, without a corresponding concern for a practice's internal goals or the demand for moral virtue. When winning is seen as the only thing that matters, sport as a practice is not only corrupted but diminished. In writing of the American sport scene, Shirley (1983, p. D1) observes:

> Our win-at-all-costs philosophy has so distorted our sense of values that we have reversed the precept of Baron Pierre de Coubertin when he founded the modern Olympic Games. Today, on all levels of sports . . . the most important thing is not merely to take part but to win: the most important thing in life is not the struggle but the triumph, the essential thing is not to have fought well but to have conquered.

A particularly reprehensible manifestation of the win-at-all-costs mentality in some forms of competitive sport is the use of violence. In many sports, writes Messner (1990, p. 203):

> the achievement of goals (i.e. winning and losing) is predicated on the successful utilisation of violence – that is, these are activities in which the human body is routinely turned into a weapon to be used against other bodies, resulting in pain, serious injury and even death.

In its most simple form violence can be characterized as a deliberate act by one player to bring about injury or pain to another player. This is sometimes done quite calculatedly in the interests of victory. When such acts are done 'to take out', 'nullify' or 'destroy' the opposition, the idea of sport as a practice is again undermined. Instead of competitive sport being an honest struggle among friendly rivals it becomes a form of antagonism between unscrupulous enemies, where there is no care or respect for the other as a person. In such an ambience opponents come to be seen as objects to be overcome, without consideration, compassion or regret. Competitive sport at this, its most defiled level, is akin to all-out war and pays no regard to the traditions, customs or codes of what a practice is. It is concerned not with honourable victory but with victory, no matter what. The win-at-all-costs approach to competitive sport is reprehensible on two counts. It is corruptive of sport in its ideal form; it is also corruptive of the moral standing of those who pursue sport in this way. From the moral point of view, therefore, the attempt to win at all costs is to be condemned.

CHEATING AND THE TAKING OF PERFORMANCE-ENHANCING DRUGS

Another reprehensible aspect of contemporary competitive sport and one which is closely tied to the syndrome of winning at all costs, is that concerned with the taking of performance-enhancing drugs. It is because this form of behaviour is normally considered as being a particularly pernicious form of cheating and an abuse of sport that it will be helpful to discuss the matter further. It will be argued, in elaboration of what has already been said about sport as a valued human practice, that the taking of such drugs is not only 'illegal' but also morally unacceptable. In order to examine this contention in some detail three separate but related arguments will be presented. The first will be called the Violation of Rules Argument. The second will be called the Unfair Advantage Argument. The third will be called the Moral Ethos Argument.

The Violation of Rules Argument

Sport, it has been argued, is a human practice that is partially characterized and governed by its rules. These can be constitutive (activity-defining), regulative (penalty-invoking) or auxiliary (eligibility-making). Without its rules a given instance of sport would not exist. A sport only comes into being as the one that it is as a result of its formulated and evolving rules. A sport's rules, so to speak, attempt to embody the purpose and possibilities of an activity by prescribing and proscribing what can and cannot be done. To wantonly disregard the rules of an activity is to disregard what is expected by those who participate in it. An activity can only retain its integrity if those who take part in it keep to the rules. If a player of a game intentionally flouts its rules that player, technically speaking, is no longer playing that game at all. Logically, he or she ceases to be a player of that game because its rules are not being followed. Put another way, the player who deliberately breaks the rules of a game ceases to be a bona fide participant in that game because the rules that define and characterize it are not being kept. This somewhat formalistically stated position, it will be appreciated, applies not only to the taking of banned drugs but to all other intentional rule-violating behaviour. It should be understood that the violation of rules argument is not just a 'legal' one but also a moral one. When a person voluntarily chooses to enter a sport he or she makes a tacit commitment to abide by the rules that are applicable. To renege upon the agreement is rather like making a promise and then not keeping it. It is not only to let oneself down but also to let down others. It is a form of dishonesty, a vice which is antithetical to the values and standards that are integral to the practice. It breaks the trust that should help mark out the type of relationship that those committed to sport as a practice should have.

Hart (1955), cited in Simmons (1979, p. 308), writing in keeping with what has been said above, comments that:

> When a number of persons conduct any joint enterprise according to rules and thus restrict their liberties, those who have submitted to these restrictions when required have a right to a similar submission from those who have benefited from their submission.

He adds that:

> The rules may provide that officials should have authority to enforce obedience ... but the moral obligation to obey the rules in such circumstances is due to the cooperating members of the society and they have the correlative moral right to obedience.

When, therefore, those governing bodies of sport, such as the International Olympic Committee or the International Tennis Federation, make rule changes, as they do from time to time, as a part of their responsibility, participants are both 'legally' and morally bound by them. When these rules concern the banning of certain drugs which fall into such classes as stimulants, narcotics, anabolic steroids, beta blockers, diuretics and peptide hormones and analogues, participants are obliged to observe them. Not to do so is to break with the condition to which all participants are tied. As long as people wish to compete in sport they are mutually bound by the rules that govern it. There is, in other words, a commitment to the practice community of which one is a member. If the rules involve the possible taking of tests, then these become a part of the rules or conditions with which all participants are expected to comply. If certain people do not wish to compete in the way the rules are laid down, they have the choice of not competing at all or competing in another forum where different rules apply. The violation of rules argument may appear somewhat arbitrary and simplistic and fly in the face of individual rights. It might be thought for instance, as some libertarians do,[1] that the athlete should have the right to decide, in accordance with the principle of informed choice and a knowledge of the harmful risks involved, about whether or not he or she should take drugs. Whilst this argument may have some moral force on grounds of individual autonomy about the conduct of a person's life in general it seems to me singularly inappropriate when applied to sport. That is to say a person cannot with consistency agree to participate in the practice and community of sport and at the same time reject some of the rules and conditions under which competition takes place.[2] To do this would be to negate the notion of fair play,[3] whereby each contestant is expected to bear an equal share of responsibility for the practice so that nobody is able to take advantage of its benefits whilst disregarding its burdens. Put simply, the intentional taking of banned drugs is a contravention of the agreed rules and is a form of cheating. Overall it can be said that cheating[4] in sport is not unlike joining a club having accepted its rules, and then, on becoming a member, disregarding them. In the same way that it is not unreasonable that a club member who flouts the rules of membership should be blackballed, so it is not unreasonable that a competitor in a sport who deliberately breaks the rules to which others subscribe should be banned from participating in it.

The Unfair Advantage Argument

Earlier it was suggested that in the practice view of sport the concept of fair play is the moral basis upon which sporting competition is predicated. Proponents of the unfair advantage argument contend that known performance enhancers such as anabolic steroids give users an unfair advantage over non-users and that in the interests of 'true' sport and 'good' competition they should not be used.

This point would remain a morally valid one not only because it breaks the rules concerning banned drugs, which it does, but because it contravenes the best traditions of sport and sportspersonship. At an intuitive level the gaining of an unfair advantage by chemically aided (drugs) or technologically aided (equipment) means, is offensive to what has been referred to as the 'good contest' in which persons come together in order to test themselves in terms of their physical prowess (speed, strength, stamina, skills, etc.) and qualities of character (courage, honesty, determination, etc.) in a spirit of friendly rivalry. The sentiment behind the unfair advantage argument is not just that the rules should be the same for all (which is what the violation of rule argument upholds) but that the preconditions and circumstances under which contestants acquire their powers (mental and physical) should not only be comparable within certain parameters but also acceptable in terms of the ethos of sport as a practice. As was made clear earlier, it is the ethos of a practice such as sport that takes us beyond a formal statement of the rules. The rules of a sport, although they may attempt to embody the ethos desired, can never entirely do so. Much is left to the moral motivation and purpose of the participants involved. The rules can be followed, but the spirit in which they were formulated may be left wanting.

What then in the light of what has been said is meant by an unfair advantage? Clearly the point at issue here is not primarily to do with whether or not all competitors have an equal chance of success (although this principle can be usefully invoked,[5] particularly perhaps in the growing years, when striking differences in height, weight, sex and background knowledge need to be taken into consideration), but is more particularly to do with whether or not a person's or team's chance of success have been improved in an ethically unacceptable manner. Gardner's (1989, p. 61) distinction between an acceptable and unacceptable unfair advantage is a helpful one. An acceptable unfair advantage is one which is unfair but none the less acceptable (or at least tolerable) within the rules and ethos of a particular sport.

Thus, if in the welterweight division of boxing one competitor has a six-inch longer reach than his opponent few people would maintain within the parameters of that competition that the advantage held was an unacceptable one, especially if he had less speed and less boxing ability. Similarly, when Steffi Graf, currently one of the world's top tennis players, owing to her genetic endowment and superior ground strokes, beats a low ranked player, few people are likely to say that her unfair advantages are unacceptable ones. They may be unfair in the sense of not being equal but they are, within the fraternity of tennis, acceptable. This, I suspect, is because nobody would wish to say that Steffi Graf in winning against her weaker opponent was in any sense being underhand. She is able to win openly, so to speak, and on her own merit. She does not break the rules nor is she clandestine in what she does.

Another category of unfair but acceptable advantage, it is sometimes alleged, involves those intentional but 'tacitly agreed' transgressions of the rules, such as tripping or holding the shirt of a player in soccer as he tries to move away with the ball. Such practices as these, it is said, are acceptable because players expect them as a 'normal' part of play. They constitute, as Leamon (1988, p. 279) puts it, 'latent agreements' and are understood by those who take part. It is sometimes argued further that because such offences involve known penalties they are looked upon as a part of the overall strategy of how the game is played. A 'skilful' player, in these circumstances, will be one who will break the rules when it is most advantageous to his side to do so. Such unfair but tacitly accepted violation of the rules, Leamon (1988, p. 281) maintains, are not cases of cheating since the players involved both expect and accept them.

Such observations as these may be descriptively correct of what actually occurs sometimes in some sports. They certainly seemed to characterize the attitude and behaviour of some teams and players, for example, in the early rounds of the 1990 and 1994 soccer World Cup. The question arises, however; are they consistent with the ethos of the practice view of sport? The answer is most certainly 'no'.[6] Are such transgressions of the rules made in any way more acceptable by the alleged fact that they are 'latently agreed'? Again, I think, the answer is most certainly 'no'. They represent interesting social/psychological data but are out of keeping with sport as an ideal human practice. Such advantage-seeking violations of the rules, I would maintain, are not only unfair and unacceptable but are also forms of cheating. This is especially so because not all rule violations are detected and can therefore be penalized in an even-handed manner in the way that the rules lay down.

It has so far been argued that some forms of unfair advantage are acceptable and other forms unacceptable. The unacceptable variety it was suggested not only arise because the rules are broken but because the method or manner by which the unfair advantage is gained is an ethically questionable one.

What then is the situation with regard to performance-enhancing drugs? Some writers think that if it can be shown that a participant's status as a person is brought into question by the taking of performance-enhancing drugs, then the idea of a fair competition no longer applies. Simon (1985, p. 11), for example, writes that 'the idea of sport is a mutual quest for excellence between *persons*' and that the whole point of athletic competition is 'to test the ability of persons, not the way bodies react to drugs'. Another expression of this statement is made by Will (1985, p. 88). He observes:

> Sport is competition to demonstrate excellence in admired activities. The excellence is more praiseworthy when the activity demands virtues of the spirit – of character – as well as physical prowess. Admirable athletic attainments involve mastery of pain and exhaustion – the triumph of character, not chemistry over adversity.

The implication of these comments is that the taking of performance-enhancing drugs not only breaks the rules of sport and is offensive to its best traditions, but in addition somehow is ethically wrong. But can the notion of 'personhood' provide an ethical justification for the banning of those drugs which, especially in some sports it would seem, give an 'unnatural' and 'artificial', and therefore unfair and unacceptable advantage to those competitors who do take them over those who do not? As Brown (1980), Gardner (1989) and others have pointed out, the problem of what a person is and how this relates to issues concerning 'body' and 'mind' and what is a 'natural' substance as opposed to an 'unnatural' one is fraught with difficulty and for the present, at least, seems to defy solution.

Rather than look to 'personhood' then as a way of offering an ethical justification for the banning of performance-enhancing drugs, I shall look instead to what I propose to call the moral ethos argument which is perhaps best seen as being complementary to both the violation of rules argument and the unfair advantage argument.

The Moral Ethos Argument

The moral ethos argument in relation to sport maintains first that the rules of sport are based upon the moral principles of universality and impartiality; and second that the ideal of sport is dependent upon those virtues such as honesty and trustworthiness that help define and sustain it. A person initiated into sport as a valued practice understands that the rules of sport are not just constitutional or functional, but moral. They are universal not only in the sense of being applicable to all people but in the sense that what is right or correct for one participant must also be considered right or correct for any other participant in the same situation. Put positively the universality principle is not unlike the Christian golden rule, 'Do unto others as you would have them do unto you.' Put negatively it is not dissimilar to the Confucian rule, 'Do not do unto others as you would not have them do unto you.' The point about the rules of sport is that they apply to all rational persons who have the ability to do the kinds of actions prohibited or required. The rules of sport, like the moral law, do not permit exceptions to be made. They apply to all who can understand them and be responsible for their actions. No one is permitted to become an exception. What applies to you also applies to me. Everyone who has been initiated into sport should have understood that they are obliged not merely to follow the rules but act in accordance with them.

The principle of impartiality emphasizes the point that the rules do not set out to favour one person or team over another. In this sense the rules are applied in a disinterested manner. Participants in sport should know and understand that in terms of the rules all participants can expect equal treatment which is applied consistently. It will be appreciated that in doing this, justice as fairness is preserved. Although most sports have umpires or referees whose job it is to apply the rules impartially, individual participants none the less are expected to apply them in a disinterested way to themselves so that they do not knowingly break or bend the rules that give them or their team an unfair advantage. What then the principle of impartiality upholds is the denial of self-interest. The common interest in the case of sport is the pursuit of a valued form of life, which has its own values and standards, in a rule-bound and morally acceptable manner. Wilson (1966, p. 123) therefore is correct when he observes that 'rules are necessary to fulfil human aims, purposes and plans'.

It will be appreciated that because a rule is applied universally and impartially this does not necessarily make it moral and it would be foolish to claim that *all* the rules of sport are moral rules. Some, as has been indicated, are concerned with description and procedure. In so far as the rules, however, are concerned with the manner in which participants should conduct themselves in relation to others, it is being claimed, they are based upon such commonly accepted moral injunctions as: don't cause pain, don't disable, don't deceive, don't cheat, keep your promise, do your duty. What is at the heart of these injunctions, or moral rules as Gert (1988, p. 284) calls them, is a respect for the participant as a person to whom consideration should be shown, not only as a person, but because the ethos of sport as a practice demands it. One mark of being in sport is to conduct oneself in a moral way and in keeping with the values, standards and best traditions of the practice.

The rules of sport then, taking into account moral injunctions as they do, are more than mores and customs. They constitute the way sports people must act if sport is to remain a practice of integrity. In the same way that all participants have rights, they also have obligations. The rules, once they have been understood and accepted as being based upon the principles of universality and impartiality, become in effect personal imperatives that are both necessary and desirable for the continuance of the practice. To be a moral agent in sport is to act willingly in accordance with the rules and the moral directives they embody. To deliberately cheat by intentionally breaking the rules is to act immorally. In principle, at least, to deliberately break the rules in order to gain an unacceptable unfair advantage is not to be in sport at all. The participant becomes both a cheat and literally a spoilsport.

What has been suggested is that the practice of sport is more than a 'social union' as outlined by Rawls (1972, p. 525) in which certain social motives and purposes are shared. It is also a moral community in which the participants are expected to conduct themselves so that the internal excellences and enjoyments can be pursued in a way that is fair and acceptable to all. In such a community, goodwill and virtue are required if its ethos is to be preserved. Goodwill is needed in order to act in accord with the rules and their moral import in a voluntary and committed manner. Virtues are needed because without them the nature and character of the practice is likely to wither and die. Goodwill involves acting with good intentions even though what is intended does not always materialize. This is why an accidental foul is not seen in the same light as an intentional one. Acting virtuously involves individual participants acting in such a way that the values, standards and best traditions of the practice are exemplified. MacIntyre (1985, p. 191) gives a clear account of what a virtue is and of its functional importance to a practice such as sport when he writes: 'A virtue is an acquired human quality, the possession and exercise of which tends to enable us to achieve those goals which are internal to practices and lack of which effectively prevents us from achieving any such goals.'

What should be clear about a virtue in relation to sport is that it is more than a disposition to act in a reliable way in given circumstances. It is a feature of what a practice is and an integral part of its ethos. Put differently, a virtue is an admired human quality which is not only conducive to the good life of man but is indispensable to those pursuits which are worthwhile. The very notion of a virtue presupposes that it is exercised in relation to a valuable form of life. Sport as an ideal practice, in keeping with its best traditions, demands from its participants that they be fair, courageous, determined, and as well as friendly, beneficent, and caring.

Virtues, in sport as elsewhere, can be considered as those forms of action which are meritorious or praiseworthy, not only in terms of how the practice is conducted, but also in terms of how they reflect upon the agent who performs them. Thus, acts of sportspersonship are a credit to sport as well as to the person who possesses them. Conversely, a vice in sport is an action that is corruptive or detrimental to the practice and to the shame of the person who possesses it. Cheats or intentional takers of performance-enhancing drugs do a disservice both to sport and to themselves.

From the moral point of view a virtue in sport is any trait or quality of character that all rational persons would advocate that all sportspersons possess. A vice is any trait or quality of character that all rational persons would advocate that no sportsperson possess. To be fair and honest in sport is not only to act in accordance with the ethos of the ideal of sport but to act virtuously in a moral way. To take an unacceptably unfair advantage or to act dishonestly in sport is to act contrary to what the ethos of sport demands and is to act in an immoral way.

In summary, the moral ethos argument shows that, although sport is a distinctive practice in so far as its skills and excellences are concerned, it is also a moral one and one in which its ethos is inseparably linked to the virtues of its individual participants. To be responsible in sport invokes the demand to be moral and to participate within a known ethos. To intentionally act otherwise is to become morally culpable. What are the implications of this argument for the particular issue of drug-taking in sport? Apart from those arguments which have been presented elsewhere[7] with regard to their possible harmful effect on athletes, the undesirable coercive pressures put on non drug-taking participants if they are to remain competitive, and the consequences that might ensue when a drug-taking sports hero becomes a role model, the question remains: Is the intentional taking of performance-enhancing drugs a moral offence against the ethos of sport as a practice? It is this question that must now be addressed if an ethical justification for the banning of them is to be provided. This is something that has not hitherto been established.

In the first argument concerned with rule violations it was suggested that when a person voluntarily enters a sport he or she tacitly agrees to accept the rules and act in accordance with them and that this was akin to the making of a promise. It was seen also that a person is not at liberty, on grounds of informed consent and personal autonomy, to disregard those particular rules pertaining to the taking of banned drugs. By choosing to enter sport, people forgo the right, it can be argued, that is their due if they had chosen not to enter it. They cannot be permitted to keep to those rules that suit them and break those that do not. They cannot both have their cake and eat it.

The weakness of Brown's (1980) libertarian argument is that he thinks athletes should be allowed to compete in sport and at the same time have the freedom to take performance-enhancing drugs. The argument of informed choice is, of course, a reasonable one in an open and free society, especially if the only one likely to be affected is the person making the choice, but it is not one, as said previously, that is appropriate in the context of sport. In choosing to participate in sport and by enjoying the benefits it bestows, the sportsman or sportswoman becomes morally bound by the rules that govern it. To break the rules by the taking of performance-enhancing drugs is not only to gain an unacceptable unfair advantage but is to break faith with those who, bound by the same rules, do not. The moral point at issue here is one of honesty – a virtue which is necessary and fundamental to all worthwhile forms of human life.

Honesty means to be straightforward and above board in one's dealings with others and not to be given to lying and cheating. Along with truthfulness and trustworthiness, honesty is a quality that not only serves socially useful functions: it is also a virtue that is necessary to sport as a practice, for without it the practice becomes tainted and corrupted.

This, I suggest, is particularly so in the case of an athlete deliberately and systematically taking performance-enhancing drugs with the intention of bringing about an advantage which he or she thinks might not have been possible but for the taking of those drugs, knowing all the time that such a choice was against the rules. Such an action, perhaps indicative of a win-at-all-costs mentality, is morally reprehensible because it amounts to a deceitful violation of trust. It involves a pretence of conforming to the rules when this in fact is not the case, while at the same time attempting to extract maximum (and unfair) advantage over others who are conforming. It is not surprising, therefore, that the word 'cheat' applies to those who, by deceit, attempt to establish an unfair advantage over fellow competitors who may be as good or even better at performing a particular task (e.g. shot-put, 800 metres run) but who, because of the circumstances, are likely, relatively speaking, to do less well. Such acts of dishonesty are not only unacceptably unfair but immoral. Athletes who choose to cheat in this way not only betray the trust of their fellow sportsmen and sportswomen and bring shame upon themselves, but also corrupt the ethos of sport itself by putting its best traditions and values in jeopardy.

The question of how what has been said so far relates to education is the subject of the next five chapters.

NOTES

1. See, for example, Brown (1980).
2. Interestingly Schneider and Butcher (1995) argue, in keeping with the idea of sport as a practice community, that the enforcement of the non-taking of performance-enhancing drugs is likely to be more effective if the athletes themselves agree about what rules to follow (Olympic athletes are being discussed here) and then seek assistance from the International Olympic Committee to implement them. This, they maintain, would overcome what they see to be 'unwarranted intrusions into the freedom and liberty of athletes' (p. 76) if a ban is made as now by the IOC without their formal agreement. Regrettably, they do not give any details about (a) how agreement would be brought about amongst athletes throughout the world, or (b) how, if agreement were possible, how enforcement could be made to be more effective than it is now.
3. Wigmore and Tuxill (1995) provide a very useful introduction to the considerations that underlie the notion of fair play in sport.
4. I am taking the term cheating to mean broadly the deliberate attempt to gain an unfair advantage. It involves such matters as intention, the violation of rules, deception, the lack of virtue and the betrayal of trust.

    Rosenburg (1995, pp. 6–8), makes a useful distinction between (a) incontest forms of cheating, which take place whilst the game is being played and (b) noncontest forms of cheating which take place before or after the game is played. The former refer primarily to the violation of constitutive and/or regulative rules by players or officials, and the latter involve the breaking of auxiliary rules such as those concerning eligibility.
5. Fraleigh (1984, p. 114), for example, refers to equal opportunity as a guide to the right action in sport.
6. Feezell (1986) also rejects the arguments of Leamon (1981) and Lehman (1981) that deliberately violating a written rule:
   1 is not necessarily morally wrong;
   2 may be a part of the game;
   3 does not entail that one is not playing the game.
7. These have been helpfully summarized by Hyland (1990, pp. 47–67).

Chapter 4

Competitive Sport, Winning and Education

The last three chapters have been concerned with the nature of sport as a valued human practice and what its moral implications are for all those who are concerned with it, whether as participants, officials, spectators or administrators. This chapter, in the light of what has been said, will examine the controversial issue of whether or not 'competitive' sport should be a part of the educational curriculum. In order to look at this matter in some detail it will be helpful first to say something about competition as a contested concept; second, to discuss the moral concerns that have been expressed about the place of competitive sport in schools; and third, to suggest ways in which the teacher can help prevent competitive sport from becoming mis-educative and instead help teach it as worthwhile practice.

COMPETITION AS A CONTESTED CONCEPT

It is sometimes said that competition is an 'essentially contested' normative concept. That is, what is understood by the term derives from incompatible value systems so that no single coherent analysis is possible.[1] Each value system makes its interpretation in accordance with what it claims to be 'convincing arguments, evidence and other forms of justification' (Gallie, 1964, p. 157). In this respect competition is like other contested concepts such as 'art' and 'democracy'. Broadly, however, it can be said that there are two views about competition: the positivist view and the negativist view. The positivist view is one that holds that competition is a precondition of personal development and social progress and that it provides a framework from which benefits and burdens can be distributed fairly and freely. Such a framework it is argued is necessary if such qualities as initiative, resource and independence are to be fostered and preserved. The negativist view, on the other hand, maintains that competitive situations threaten cooperative ventures and help undermine worthwhile personal and social relationships and form a vicious distinction between winners and losers. Competition, it is said, is often the source of envy, despair, selfishness, pride and callousness.

When these ideologically opposed views about competition are discussed in the context of education it is perhaps not surprising that there are those who are for it and those who are against it. Prvulovich (1982, pp. 82–3), for example, a supporter of competition, writes:

> Competition can and does bring out new talents, often undreamt of, and in its various forms caters for different abilities, talents and skills. Moreover it encourages new ventures, and whets the appetite for more knowledge and deeper self-fulfilment.

Conversely, Fielding (1976, p. 140), who is a representative of the negativist view, writes:

> I reject the use of competition in schools: competition as a social ideal seems to me abhorrent; competition as a procedural device is morally repugnant because whatever other criteria one wishes to include or omit I would insist that part of one's characterisation contains some reference to working against others in a spirit of selfishness.

Dearden (1976, p. 114), perhaps in an effort to provide a neutral analytic account of competition in the face of general value-laden statements such as those above, posits three separately necessary and jointly sufficient conditions for A and B to be in competition for X:

1. 'A and B must both want X. There must be some common object desired by both.'
2. 'A's gaining of X must exclude B's gaining possession of it.'
3. 'Both A and B should persist in trying to gain exclusive possession of X even when they know that one of them must be excluded.'

This 'simplifying scheme' of Dearden's, as he calls it, although helpful to a point, omits too many other relevant considerations to be of universal use. It has been criticized by Fielding (1976) on two main grounds. The first is that the 'essentialist methodology' (i.e. one that attempts to characterize competition by identifying a set of logically necessary and sufficient conditions) is just too simplistic. Each condition, he maintains, because of the value-ladened nature of the term can be 'sensibly challenged' (p. 126). The point here is that an essentialist methodology is inappropriate to the task of characterizing competition because it cannot be done whilst remaining impartial to one of the rival views on offer. The second of Fielding's criticisms is on substantive ground (i.e. in terms of what is both raised and more particularly omitted in discussion about the use of the term).[2] He also makes the point that it is also important when dealing with an appraisive concept such as competition that some attention be given to its historical career. He quotes MacIntyre (1971, p. 95) in support of the view that: 'we cannot investigate a philosophical subject matter adequately unless we take seriously the fact that such a subject matter always has a historical dimension. That dimension is missing in most work by philosophers in the analytic tradition'.

It is because I consider all three points not only valid in relation to Dearden's analysis of competition, but more importantly it is because they are necessary to an understanding of competition in sport in the context of education that they will be borne in mind in the sections that follow.

COMPETITIVE SPORT AND EDUCATION

Meakin (1982), in taking account of both Dearden's and Fielding's work on competition, examines what he presents as being the 'strong' and 'weak' critiques that are often levelled against the moral desirability of having competitive sport as a part of the compulsory educational curriculum. It is proposed to look at each of these in turn.

The Strong Critique and an Answer to It

The strong critique against competition in schools, especially when it is compulsory, is that competition *per se* is wrong. The claim is that it is intrinsically immoral and leads to selfish and egotistical forms of behaviour. Competitive sport is often seen as a prime example of these tendencies and as a result attracts a good deal of moral censure. As Meakin (1981, p. 59) expresses it:

> The target of this censure is the undesirable behaviour of many competitors; a bad temperedness that often erupts into violence, a petulant reluctance to accept decisions of umpires and referees, a tendency to bend the rules and commit outright fouls and, more generally, an unsportsmanlike behaviour towards opponents.

The strong case against competitive sport in schools then is that it is inherently immoral and that it causes and reinforces undesirable social values and conduct.

Before examining this view of competitive sport it would be helpful if some general comments were made about the involvement or otherwise of compulsion in relation to competition in the context of education. Two points are of underlying importance. The first, as has previously been indicated, is that normally moral choices are free choices. The question arises therefore whether curriculum subjects, if they are made compulsory, are in keeping with morality and moral education? On the face of it, it would seem not. If what is considered important in learning and education is not made compulsory, however, how can educational aims and objectives be rationally implemented? It is of course possible to take the view that education can and should proceed on the basis that only when a pupil is attracted to a subject or has agreed willingly to enter into it that it should be taught. The difficulties of holding this view are too well known to warrant explication here. Two points can none the less be briefly made. The first is that some pupils may never be attracted to a given subject no matter what efforts are made to point out its intrinsic or instrumental values. Should it therefore just be disregarded? The second point is that in any case, the only way of finding out whether a subject has something about it that is rewarding or beneficial in some way, is to try it by engaging in it. An alternative view is that it is only by initiating pupils into what are considered the worthwhile activities of a culture compulsorily, if necessary, at least up to a given age, can they later make a responsible and informed choice about what they most want to do. As White (1982, p. 132) observes, in order to become free a pupil 'must pass through a period of compulsory education'. It is only when a sufficient grounding has been given in a range of selected pursuits that a pupil is able to make a free and more informed choice about whether or not he or she wishes to carry on with them.

It seems to me that the latter of these two views is the more sound, both on moral and pragmatic grounds. In principle and in practice it is likely to prove the more secure way of promoting the interests of a pupil's educational growth and development.

Returning to the main question of competition, it will be recalled that it is often important to provide some historical perspective on how a term has come to be used and understood. This is certainly the case in relation to sport. Originally, com-petitio meant 'to question, to strive together'. It was more closely tied to friendship than to rivalry. Competition in the context of sport was, and for many still is, seen as a struggle for excellence,[3] a form of excellence that would not be possible were it not for the type of situation that sport provides. To compete in sport, as has previously been pointed out, it is first necessary to understand the activity and agree to abide by the rules which govern it. If a competitor deliberately breaks or flouts the rules it can be seriously questioned whether what is done remains sport. The point here is that competitive sport is not an unbridled form of conflict, as it is sometimes depicted, but a rule-governed institutionalized practice which attempts to regulate what is permitted and not permitted along lines that are just to all. Additionally, it is reinforced by a set of social conventions and codes of behaviour that are traditionally expected to form a part of a 'sporting' competition. Paradoxically, competitive sport is best exemplified as being a rule-governed form of friendly rivalry, which involves cooperation. Perry's (1975, p. 128) observation that 'competitions require us to assume the capacity to co-operate if they are to run at all' is perhaps particularly true of sporting ones. To say, therefore, that a game is competitive does not necessarily mean that cooperation between the two contestants or two sides is absent; rather it demands that it is present, at least in some degree, if competitive sport as an institutional practice is to continue.

It is perhaps in the long-standing movement known as Olympism that the approach to competitive sport is best enshrined. It stresses the ethic of fair play and sportspersonship and upholds the view that competition should be marked by honest endeavour and goodwill. Far from seeing competitive sport as immoral and antisocial, it sees it as a form of contest that generates fellowship in a mutual struggle for excellence. This picture of competitive sport, it will be seen, is something of an ideal but it is one which has been and remains a part of the story of competitive sport. Whether or not this ideal is lived out as a part of a young person's upbringing is largely, if not entirely, a matter of how competitive sport is promoted and taught in schools. What then is being rejected, both on conceptual and historical grounds, is the view that competitive sport is inherently and therefore necessarily immoral.

The Question of Selfishness

A serious charge that remains, however, is that competitive sport leads to selfish behaviour. It will be recalled that Fielding (1976, pp. 140–1) rejected competition in schools on the grounds that it led 'to working against others in a spirit of selfishness'. Now, although in terms of an outcome of a game, it can be said that one person's victory is another person's defeat, or alternatively, one person's gain is another's loss, does it follow that selfishness is involved?

In view of what has already been said the answer to this must surely be 'no'. First, as has already been noted, competitive sport takes place within a framework of constitutive rules which are applicable to all participants. These rules are aimed at safeguarding the interests of everyone by being fair. Second, the ideal of 'the good competition', which is perhaps best characterized by acts of sportspersonship, demands not only that individual competitors play fairly in accordance with the rules but that they act as much in the interests of others as themselves. Unless all participants agree to cooperate in these respects, sport as a valued human practice will cease to exist.

It will be noted that the conceptual points just made about what competitive sport is, not only help refute the view that it is inherently immoral, but when taken together provide normative criteria by which appraisals in relation to conduct in sport can take place. Without a clear identification of what competitive sport is and should be, little can be done about evaluating it as it is actually practised.

What has been argued is that the practice view of sport is not, by virtue of the fact that it is competitive, necessarily selfish. This is, of course, not to deny that the motivations of some individual participants may not be selfish. A competitor in sport, as in other walks of life, may be concerned about his or her own interests to the exclusion of the interests of others. The captain of a men's cricket team, for example, may be so concerned about scoring a hundred runs himself that he does not declare before he has done so, thus forgoing the chance of his team winning the match. A rugby centre three-quarter may be so intent on scoring the winning try himself that he denies his wing the chance of securing victory for the team. Such acts, of course, are selfish and they are not considered in keeping with good sportsperson-like behaviour.

What can be concluded from the above discussion is that the idea of competitive sport neither encourages selfishness nor condones it. When it does occur it is generally condemned both on grounds of principle as well as on grounds of being non-efficacious to the purpose in hand.

The Question of Winning

A further aspect of the strong critique against competitive sport is the question of winning. In order to look at this more fully, in relation to what has already been said, it will be convenient to outline and then comment upon an article by Bailey (1975) in which he attacks and condemns the point of winning in the playing of games. It is of particular interest in this context because it raises a number of other issues of concern to the educationist that can be profitably discussed.

Bailey begins his article by expressing doubts about the 'appropriateness of competitive games as a part of compulsory general education'.[4] He is particularly sceptical of the view 'that competitive games are generally educative' (p. 40) and that they 'generate a kind of moral and character-building spin-off' (p. 41). In drawing upon a passage from Caillois (1961) he accepts as a basis for argument that competitive games make winning the 'point of the whole enterprise' (p. 40), that the paradigm case for playing games would be playing to win, that the rules are there 'solely to the end of making the claim to have won beyond any dispute' (p. 41), in order that players can 'demonstrate their superiority over other individuals or groups' (p. 43).

Bailey's objections then to the inclusion of competitive games (sports) in education stems from the fact that he sees competitive games as being tied to the notion of winning. He wants to maintain on account of this that their point lies in beating the opposition in order to demonstrate an unquestioned superiority. What is particularly worrying to Bailey from the 'moral' point of view is that in teaching games 'we are teaching those behaviours and attitudes conducive to the defeat of the other side' (1975, p. 43). He maintains that 'since winning is the essential objective, then infringements of rules and penalties become a part of the calculation as to whether an action is towards or away from winning' (p. 43). What is implied here is that the rules of games are merely technical and functional and not moral (p. 47). He adds that if competitive games are made compulsory this takes us further still from the idea of freedom upon which morality and moral education depends. Bailey concludes from his account of the connection between education and competitive games, especially if they are made compulsory, that we must 'not only abandon the idea that participation in competitive games morally educates, but we must accept the idea that educationally we should seek to diminish, rather than encourage, the importance of competing and winning' (p. 48).

On the face of it, Bailey's reservations about the place of games in education seem plausible, yet a closer examination of them reveals a misunderstanding of what competitive games in the form of rugby, soccer, hockey and cricket and so on, are (or should be) all about. Indeed, he is so committed to the idea of winning as being 'the point of the whole enterprise' that this colours and distorts much else of what he has to say.

To maintain of games, as Bailey does, that winning is the point of playing them is to misunderstand why people participate in them. Bailey seems to think that if he can attack and undermine the notion and motive of winning in games he will condemn any worthiness there is in playing them. By concentrating upon the point of winning he not only misconstrues the nature of sporting competition but draws from this a number of questionable conclusions. Comment first of all will be made about Bailey's contention that winning is 'the point of the whole enterprise'.

It would be correct to say that once a game is underway it would not be much of a game if the players did not try to win but it would be quite wrong to assume from this that winning is the sole point of playing them. *Trying to win* then may be considered a necessary feature of competing, but this is not to be confused with a person's reason or motive for playing. For many schoolchildren (as well as for many adults) winning is a prospect rarely achieved but this does not prevent them wanting and continuing to compete and trying to win. Their reason for playing may be to do with fun, fitness, therapy, friendship, sociability or the pursuit of excellence, rather than winning in order to 'demonstrate their superiority over others'.

If, as Thompson (1975, p. 150) points out, 'the only point of a competitive game is to win then the only criterion for choosing to play a game is that one's chances of winning are high', a person would only participate in those games where this is the case. He or she would deliberately seek out weak opponents in order to be sure of winning every time. Clearly if this were the case the practice of sport would become absurd. The idea of 'the good contest' or 'the good game' as a reason for competing would cease to exist.[5] What is clear is that although competitive games involve the prospect of producing 'winners' and 'losers', it does not follow that winning is the sole point of playing them. Nor does it follow that their value lies only in being victorious. Weiss (1969, p. 183), for example, reminds us that:

> Even the defeated gain from a game. They benefit from the mere fact that they have engaged in a contest, that they have encountered a display of great skill, that they have made the exhibition of that skill possible or desirable, that they have exerted themselves to the limit, and that they have made a game come to be.

Again, according to Delattre (1975, p. 135), it is in the testing rather than in victory that the source of value in competition in sport lies. He writes:

> The testing of one's mettle in competitive athletics is a form of self discovery ... The claim of competitive athletics to importance rests squarely on their providing us opportunities for self-discovery, for concentration and intensity of involvement, for being carried away by the demands of the contest ... with a frequency seldom matched elsewhere ... This is why it is a far greater success in competitive athletics to have played well under pressure of a truly worthwhile opponent and lost than to have defeated a less worthy or unworthy one where no demands were made.

It will be seen then that from the point of view of personal development more can sometimes be learnt from losing than from winning. The player of games, like the politician or business executive, has to learn to cope with disappointment as well as with triumph without being unduly affected by either.

By insisting that the only point of playing a game is to win, Bailey rules out any intrinsic value it might have. As Dunlop (1975, p. 156) observes: 'What is logically necessary (for a competitive game to take place) is not necessarily really important in the sense that it must be the "central" aim of the player or team.'

What surely above all else the teacher wants to bring about is not a vicious and degenerate form of competitiveness, which is concerned with demonstrating superiority and winning at all costs, but the bringing into being of a 'good game' so that all players can both profit from it and enjoy it. The emphasis here is not on the end result – winning or losing – but rather on what takes place and the manner in which it takes place. The intelligent use of mastered skills, the well executed tactic, the perceptive employment of strategy, the disciplined blending of team effort are but some of the facets of what makes up the content of a good game. When it comes to the manner in which a game is played a good teacher will be concerned with getting children to understand and willingly abide by the rules, follow their spirit, develop such admired qualities as courage and determination as well as to conduct themselves in a friendly and sportsmanlike way. Trying to win is a part of what it is to have a good game but the result of winning or losing is always subservient to the values inherent in playing a game well. When a game is played well, in the right spirit and the participants learn and derive pleasure from it, neither winning nor losing assumes undue importance. When competitive games are played along these lines, as they should be within an educational setting, it will be seen that many perjorative assumptions about the nature of competition disappear. Instead of seeing winning as the point in the playing of games with all the negative undertones this often induces, it becomes possible to see them as human activities, as miniature forms of life, which provide a framework within which physical abilities can be developed and performed, qualities of character fostered and friendly forms of conduct encouraged. A competitive game, as Dearden (1976, p. 121) acknowledges, can still be a good one even if one loses. Its value lies in what occurs in the process of playing it rather than in its result. What seems clear is that the ethos or manner in which a game is seen and approached can be influenced by those who teach it.

In summary, it has been argued that Bailey's view of competition in relation to sport, especially in an educational context, is misconceived. It is misconceived because it fails to appreciate that the historical and normative framework associated with sport is essentially an ethical one. This, of course, is not to say that some of the concerns Bailey expresses are not real ones or that such acts as selfishness, cheating and fouling will not sometimes occur. The point to be refuted here, and the one upon which Bailey rests his case, is that because sport is necessarily competitive it is necessarily immoral. It mistakes the idea of competitive sport for certain aspects of abuse that can sometimes occur within it.

The Weak Critique and the Role of the Teacher

Unlike the strong critique the weak critique does not see competition as inherently wrong but only contingently so. Meakin (1986, p. 64) writes that: 'the weak critique of competitive sport is that, while not morally wrong in itself, such sport is generally practised in morally undesirable ways.' Censure in this case is not so much directed at competition itself but at the abuses which often accompany it. What in effect is being criticized is not competition *per se* but the manner in which it sometimes takes place whether it is to do with violence, intentional rule infringements or generally objectionable ways of behaving. Often, it is said, the young in seeing some of the more unsavoury attitudes and habits depicted by their heroes in senior or professional teams come to imitate them, thinking that, even if their behaviour is not praiseworthy, it is the generally expected thing to do.

The problem posed by the weak critique then, is not how to abolish competition because it is thought irredeemably harmful but how to safeguard it from becoming corrupted. The prime question for the school is how to initiate pupils into competitive sports and athletics without them picking up undesirable attitudes and offensive forms of behaviour or, if they do, what can be done about rectifying the situation. Clearly the teacher has an important role to play here. What then can be done to prevent competitive sport becoming a potential source of miseducation or more positively a form of education in which moral values are instantiated? A number of approaches are possible. Three are listed below and each will be considered in turn.

1.   Altering the value orientation.
2.   Making a systematic appeal to rationality.
3.   Being an exemplar of the ideals to which a commitment has been made.

Each of these will be briefly explicated and discussed as to their educational acceptability.

Altering the Value Orientation

The view of sport that has been previously explicated which I have referred to as the practice view, is one that is best characterized as an ethically based rule-governed institutionalized social practice marked by competitive whole-bodied but friendly rivalry intrinsic to which is a sense of fair play and sportspersonship. On this view to speak of sport means to speak of competition. The one is a part of the other. Without competition sport would not be what it is. In recent years, however, the phrase 'competitive sport' has been used to connote a 'serious' undertaking of sport in contradistinction to a 'non-serious' or 'recreational' approach. Some educationists having noted the distinction being made here, have argued that school sport should be designated 'recreational sport' in an effort to detract from its essentially competitive nature. Whilst one can appreciate the motives for a change in orientation it seems to me misguided. Sport, like mathematics or history, is what it is, and is not to be confused with whether it is found to be recreative or can be taught in a recreative way. The educational justification for sport forming a part of the movement curriculum is that it is thought to be worthwhile in itself, not because if may be found to have recreative value, even though this may be fortuitously the case. This point is not always understood by those who wish to transform the traditional view of sport, which is intrinsically competitive, into something else. If the teacher understands the nature of sport sufficiently well and is committed to it, the Lombardian ethic[6] – where winning at all costs is emphasized to the detriment of social and moral values – will not be allowed to develop. What the teacher should be able to control, and condemn, which conversely the professional team manager may sometimes encourage, is the attempt to gain victory by unfair and immoral means.

   An equally misguided approach that can be adopted to overcome or prevent sport being practised in undesirable ways is to see it as a means or a vehicle through which social and moral values can be taught and reinforced. Although sport, as has been maintained is inherently concerned with social values and moral qualities, which the teacher may profitably point out relate to life as well as sport, it damages the integrity and educational justification of sport if it is seen and used as but an instrument in the service of the moral educator. The case against this approach toward sport, which largely coincides with what Kew (1978) has called the 'radical ethic',[7] is that it subverts and detracts from sport as being worthwhile in itself.

   A similar criticism can be made of what has been called the 'counter culture' approach to sport. In an attempt to overcome the Lombardian ethic, with its overemphasis on winning, it has attempted to promote the idea that 'playing is everything; the end result is unimportant'. In its simplest form, Kew (1978, p. 109) remarks that it is 'an approach in which games playing is regarded as pure fun and enjoyment, a love of moving and exercising skill along with other people'. Again sport is not seen in terms of itself, but as a means to something outside itself. This something is not altogether clear but seems to be associated with the notion of authentic existence which is concerned with the 'immediacy of experience, with the here and now, with the process rather than the product' (p. 111).

   The problem with all of the above attempts to alter the centrality of competitiveness in sport by orientating it in a different direction, and in so doing reducing it to a form of instrumentalism, is that it no longer remains sport, certainly, at least, in its traditional sense.

Making a Systematic Appeal to Rationality

If as the traditional or practice view suggests competitive sport is constituted and governed by rules which logically presuppose fundamental moral principles, such as equality and a respect and concern for the interests of others, what can the educationist do to aid and supplement the process which should be a part of his teaching?

Meakin (1981, p. 246) suggests that discussion, both formal and informal, should be a part of the teaching process: 'The aim would be to sensitise the developing child to the moral presuppositions of competitive sport and bring home to him that he has some degree of choice whether to abide (by them) or not.' The teacher, he suggests, should not only ask children whether they ought or want to behave in certain ways but, by an appeal to moral reasoning, should condemn 'bad' practices and recommend 'good' ones. Thus, in a rational way, can the development of ethical ideals and modes of conduct such as modesty in victory and dignity in defeat be built up. This, if handled intelligently, could be of assistance in the prevention of antisocial and morally wrong practices, perhaps even in the encouragement and living out of what is demanded by the practice view of sport. This, however, on its own is not likely to be sufficient. It could, if not related back to sportsfield practice, result in an intellectual acceptance of what is appropriate behaviour without it necessarily occurring. As was intimated earlier, being moral is a matter of maturation, character and conduct as much as reason.

Another rational approach to teaching sport in schools, suggests Wilson (1986), is to get children to understand that some activities like sport, chess and debating are by their very nature competitive and that it is foolish to argue that just because something is competitive it is necessarily morally harmful. On the contrary, he suggests trying to meet the inherent standards of an activity is a form of competition, be it to do with mathematics, speaking a language or being an athlete. In each of these endeavours it is realistic to expect that some pupils will be better at some activities than others and to recognize and accept that this is a part of growing up. What should be made clear from the moral point of view, however, is that whether they are 'successful' or 'unsuccessful' the teacher retains his or her respect for them as persons.

Being an Exemplar of the Ideals to Which a Commitment Has Been Made

If, as has been suggested, social and moral conduct in sport arises not so much from understanding the rules and the principles upon which they are based, but in the dispositions and attitudes cultivated and practised, it follows that rational discussion, whilst helpful, is on its own not sufficient. What perhaps is needed in the sphere of sport, no less than other areas of the curriculum, is that pupils perceive what is required of them. If children are able to see what it is to act honestly, fairly, bravely, resolutely and generously, in competition they are more likely to be impressed by such acts than by a discussion of them.

Rationality then, is one thing but manifestations of virtue are another. Acts of sportspersonship are more likely to fire the imagination and do more for the ideals of sport than any amount of casuistry. That is why it is important that teachers, the guardians of the best traditions of sport, should be conscious of their role, for it is they who set the standards that those in their care are likely to follow. They should understand that how to conduct oneself on the sportsfield is likely to be as much caught as taught. It is not enough then, that teachers be a clear interpreter of the rules of sport. What is required in addition is to show themselves as being genuinely committed to the forms of consideration and conduct it demands. It is unlikely that social and moral values in sport can be effectively taught unless teachers show a commitment to such values themselves. This is, of course, a tall order yet it is not an impossible one to fulfil. It is because of the power of example and commitment that it becomes all the more necessary, in the words of Warnock (1977, pp. 135–6), 'for teachers to know what they are at, what characteristics they are displaying, since their virtues and vices will form a part of the whole picture of possible moral behaviour that a child will, gradually, build up'. In being conscious of their role, however, it is as well for them to remember Ryle's (1975, p. 57) comment that: '... in matters of morality as distinct from techniques, good examples had better not be set with edifying purpose'. The point here is that if teachers are too intent or heavy-handed in the presentation of themselves as a model, or are seen not to be genuine, they are likely to be scorned, ridiculed or perhaps even worse, disregarded. In the last resort sports teachers' work is measured not so much by their pupils' dispassionate judgements but by the attitudes and conduct of the pupils as they engage in the fervour and challenge of competition.

NOTES

1. Fielding (1976, p. 135) suggests that an 'essentially contested' concept is one about which disputes do not resolve themselves even when the contestants are aware of rival interpretations. Indeed, disputants seek to establish further arguments and justifications to back up their claims in order to establish even more firmly their own particular interpretation. In this kind of situation some philosophers have tended to take the view that the issues are resolvable and that resolution is likely to be brought about by examining the metaphysical presuppositions of the participants. However, Gallie, who first coined the notion of an essentially contested concept, suggests that, although endless disputes do remain endless precisely because of metaphysical or indeed psychological recalcitrance, this need not necessarily be the case. With certain concepts that are central to aesthetics, political philosophy and philosophy of religion, these apparently endless disputes:

   > are perfectly genuine: (and) although not resolvable by argument of any kind, are nevertheless sustained by perfectly respectable argument and evidence ... These mutually contesting, mutually contested uses of the concept (make) up its standard general use. (Gallie, 1956, p. 169)

2. Fielding (1976, pp. 126–9) cites as omissions: the relationship between competition and regulation; the nature of the regulation; whether competition is object-centred or opponent-centred; whether it is voluntary or involuntary; whether reference is being made to the competitive process or the competitive motive.

3. Simon (1985, p. 28), for example, writes that competition in the context of sports can be defended on the grounds that it is 'a mutually acceptable quest for excellence'.

4. Although Bailey's (1975) article refers to games, he is really talking about those competitive activities called sports. For the purpose of this section I have left his terminology as it is.
5. Comments by Arnold and Fraleigh are of interest here. Fraleigh (1984, chapters 8 and 9) writes that the good contest shall be in part characterized by such ethical considerations as equal opportunities for optimal performance, non-injurious action, non-harassment, courtesy and sympathetic regard. Arnold (1979, p. 161) refers to the 'good contest' as having three separate but inter-related aspects: 'the good strife, the creation and discharge of enjoyable tension and the aesthetic living out of skills and strategies'.
6. The Lombardian ethic is so called because it derives from a famous American football coach Vince Lombardi, who is reported to have said, 'winning is not the most important thing; it's the only thing'. It is of interest to note that what Lombardi is claimed to have actually said is, 'winning isn't everything, but wanting to win is'. See Morris (1979).
7. The radical ethic is perhaps best exemplified by the English Public Schools of the mid-nineteenth century which used sports as a means of social and moral reinforcement. See Kew (1978, p. 104).

Chapter 5

Sport, Fairness and the Development of Character

In Chapter 4 it was argued against some of its critics that competitive sport is neither logically nor necessarily contingently antithetical to moral education. It was suggested in fact that if taught in an enlightened way it can actually contribute to its advancement. This chapter will pursue further this last point and will argue that when sport is understood as a valued human practice, as it should be in schools, it is inherently concerned with the moral and, as has been shown, both demands and cultivates those principles and virtues that are the basis of a morally educated person. In order to elaborate upon this, it is proposed, first, to say something about the claims that have been made in the past about the relationship between character development and physical activity, second, to explicate what is meant by character in the context of education, third, to make clear what fairness in sport entails in the form of underlying social principles and fourth, to examine how sport can provide opportunities for the development of a moral character.

PAST CLAIMS ABOUT CHARACTER DEVELOPMENT

There is a long and respected tradition that upholds the view that there is an important relationship between a person's physical life and the development and formation of his or her character. In the *Republic* Plato (1955) condemns an education which is exclusively academic just as roundly as he condemns one which is exclusively physical. The first he says produces people who are 'soft and sensitive'; the other who are 'tough and uncivilised'. What is needed, he suggests, is a combination of the two elements in order 'to produce a mind that is civilised and brave, as opposed to cowardly and uncivilised' (pp. 145–55). In Rousseau's *Emile* a similar note is struck. It is as with Plato, a matter of the body for the sake of the soul. 'Give his body constant exercise, make it strong and healthy in order to make him good and wise.' 'A feeble body makes a feeble mind.' 'The weaker the body the more imperious its demands; the stronger it is the better it obeys.' (pp. 21–33, 82–4). These are but some of the aphorisms that poured from the pen of Rousseau and indicate something of his conviction that the physical life and the development of character were somehow intertwined.

It is to nineteenth century Britain, however, that we must turn if we are to more fully understand the contention that there is a relationship between the playing of games and the formation of character. It was here in certain of the English Public Schools that the cult of athleticism was forged. It was a term which not merely signified a liking for team games in particular but extolled their efficacy as a means of character education. If today few people would look to the playing fields of Britain's schools with such unabashed confidence at the assumptions then being made, it should be remembered that the type of character envisaged was based on the ideal of a muscular-Christian gentleman which was at the same time religious in its zeal and imperialistic in its demands. 'The formation of the Christian character' writes Mangan (1975) 'was the self-declared role of the institution.' This, however, was tempered by the fact that it was functionally related to the expansion of empire and called for 'the production of self-confident, hardy soldiers, administrators and ... missionaries' who would be 'capable of withstanding the physical and psychological rigours of imperial duty' (pp. 148–9).

During this period team games came to be regarded as a highly important means whereby such traits as courage, loyalty and cooperation were cultivated. Of the connection between the playing of games and the development of character neither the schools themselves nor others outside them were in doubt. Charles Kingsley, for example, wrote:

> that games conduce, not merely daring and endurance but better still temper, self-restraint, fairness, honour, unenvious approbation of another's success, and all that 'give and take' of life which stands a man in such good stead when he goes forth into the world and without which, indeed, his success is always maimed and partial.[1]

The influential Clarendon Commission which reported on the Public Schools in 1864 found that among other virtues it was partially 'their love of healthy sport and exercise' that helped 'in the moulding of the character of the English Gentleman'.[2] At Oxford, Bishop Selwyn recognized that the Christian character had a quite explicit physical dimension when he asserted of physical activities that:

> they are a training of the future man for higher purposes than mere playing at cricket, or pulling a boat. It is part of that moral training through physical processes which is necessary that man might be finished for good works.[3]

These publicly professed beliefs were by no means confined to Britain. By the turn of the twentieth century they had extended to the Commonwealth as well as to many other parts of the world. In the United States, for example, Hussey (1938, p. 578) wrote in the *American Educational Review* that:

> Athletics [referring to competitive sports] offer the greatest opportunity for character development of any activity. The fundamentals of character are gained through participation in sports under right leadership, and a person who lacks these fundamentals may be sensitive, refined and cultured but will lack the vital character qualities most needed and esteemed by this society.

More recently this same belief in the value of sport as a preparation for life and possibly battle are echoed in the words of General Douglas MacArthur (quoted by Hoch, 1972, p. 72) who wrote:

Upon the fields of friendly strife
Are sown the seeds
That, upon other fields, on other days,
Will bear the fruits of victory.

What then is to be made of the purported and assumed relationship between sport and the development of character? Empirically the matter would be hard to settle.[4] It may well be that in the nineteenth century the ideology of athleticism was not sufficiently examined and that this is why its claims in more recent decades have been properly brought into question by some and either refuted or ridiculed by others. Conceptually, however, I think the relationship between sport and the notion of a moral character is stronger than some critics allow. This will be demonstrated in the sections that follow.

CHARACTER AND EDUCATION

Character, it can be said, involves more than socialization. It implies that a person is actively involved in what he or she thinks and does and is not merely the passive recipient of other people's thoughts or behaviour. The person who has character is one who is able to make independent choices and judgements in accordance with reason and has the strength of will, if necessary, to carry them out in what he or she does. The person who has moral character will act in the light of considered principles in a rational and justifiable way. He or she will respect and show concern equally for others, will demonstrate the possession of such virtues as honesty and integrity and will, if necessary, act with courage and in a way that is responsible and appropriate to the context or situation at hand.

What perhaps needs to be clear is that character, especially when used in its moral sense, is not to be confused with the term personality. Personality, according to Quinton (1982, pp. 21–6), is concerned with how a person presents himself or herself to the world. This may change from time to time, whereas character is more concerned with those relatively enduring and stable thoughts and actions that make the person the individual he or she essentially is. Character, then, is more associated with a person possessing certain values and beliefs and having a long-term and meaningful commitment to them.

Lickona (1992, p. 51) speaks of good character as what we would ideally like for our children. He associates it with Aristotle's claim that it is the life of right conduct in relation to his own and other people's welfare and long-term interests. He maintains that good character can be conceived as having three interrelated parts: moral knowing, moral feeling and moral behaviour. It becomes operative when such self-oriented virtues as self-control and moderation, and other-oriented virtues such as generosity and compassion are lived out in our everyday lives so that they become habits of the mind, of the heart and of action. As Lickona expresses it: 'Good character consists of knowing the good, desiring the good and doing the good.' Moral knowing comprises a number of related processes including those of being aware of certain situations, having a language (e.g. honesty, responsibility, tolerance, etc.) that applies to them and being able to make judgements about what best to do. Moral feeling involves such emotionally infused states as conscience, self-esteem and empathy as well as self-control. Moral action, if it is to be effective, must be guided by knowing how to go about it (i.e. competence) and having the resolve to carry it through.

Kant (1991), in his reflections on education, recognized that there is more to education than book learning. He believed strongly that the essential thing about education is the formation of the person by his or her own efforts in terms of the person's talents and character (pp. 2–3). For him the commandment to live in accordance with nature paves the way for the commandment to go beyond nature by the exercise of reason in terms of duty and law (p. 108). For Kant the primary end of education is the development of moral character. If this is to be achieved each pupil must not only be accorded respect by others by being seen as an end and never merely as a means but also by the cultivation of self-respect. When children (or any other people) lie, they degrade themselves by robbing themselves of the dignity and trust that every person should have (p. 102). Lying, cheating and other forms of taking advantage of another are not only to be regretted in social terms but also in terms of the moral damage it does to their own character. It will be argued shortly that such self-demanding acts are as applicable in the sphere of sport and games as in other spheres of life for, like other activities, they are both social and personal in nature. Lying and cheating are to be condemned just as much as honesty and fair play are to be upheld for they affect the self-respect of the person just as they affect the quality of relations with others. Kant did not see the formation of character as something happening overnight but rather as something that emerges from the constant and prolonged process of self-formation. It is marked by a steadfast pursuit of purpose based upon reasoned and universal moral principles. It is of interest here that Peter's (1981, p. 29) depiction of 'having character', which emphasizes the regulation of conduct in accordance with high order principles, is very much in keeping with this last point. He comments that character traits differ from other sorts of traits in that the former 'are shown in the sort of things a man can decide to be' (p. 25). He goes on that this may sometimes 'be a matter of forcing himself to do something in the face of social pressures or persistent temptations' (p. 25). What then is being upheld here is that individuals who have character are able to will themselves to do what is considered right even in the face of difficulties or inclinations to do otherwise. In this, and in accordance with Kant's views, the term character when attributed to a person is not merely to describe that person but to morally praise him or her. It is to recognize that the person has taken a hand in becoming perfect as a moral being and has been, importantly, concerned with his or her own moral development.

Overall it will be seen that the Aristotelian approach to character with its emphasis on the virtues is somewhat different from the Kantian one with its insistence upon the adoption of universal principles. Whereas for Aristotle (1973) the notion of character is based upon what is required to promote human development and welfare in ourselves and others by the cultivation and exercise of the virtues of character education, Kant (1991, p. 85) is more concerned with 'the disposition of the will by which a person binds himself to certain practical principles which he sets permanently before himself by his own reason'. It will be seen that in so far as the practice of sport is concerned, however, there is no conflict between the two traditions. This is so because, as will be shown, sport is the type of practice that is not only based upon the notion of fairness and its reference to the twin principles of freedom and equality but is also dependent, as has been shown, upon the cultivation and employment of such virtues as honesty and courage, for without them it would become vulnerable to corruption and thus be in danger of undermining its own values and the pursuit of its own internal goods.

What then, in general, should be understood is that the notion of character in its moral sense, as Wright (1971, p. 203) observes, cannot be defined 'through an inventory of actions performed, as by a description of the principles that give coherence and meaning to an individual's behaviour, and of the relatively enduring dispositions that underly it'.

Kant's views on the relationship between education and the formation of character are of underlying importance to sport in at least three respects. First, it is seen as a moral one based upon reasoned and universal principles. Second, it emphasizes the giving of respect to others as well as having respect for oneself. Third, it draws attention to the fact that the development of character is not a passive process but an autonomously active and purposeful one to do with self-formation. All these points I want to uphold when it comes to sport and conduct appropriate to it. Before tackling this task more specifically, however, it will be helpful to look at the ethical basis of sport which, in keeping with what has been said, will be depicted as a distinctive form of practice concerned quintessentially with fairness.

SPORT AS FAIRNESS

The idea and practice of sport is concerned with justice as fairness. Rawls (1958, p. 165), in speaking of justice as fairness, although he is predominantly concerned with the social practice of institutions, recognizes that there is a distinction but none the less a connection between the application of the term fairness to a practice and the application of that term to a particular action by an individual. In his book *A Theory of Justice* he explicates his theory of 'fairness' by reference to two principles: freedom and equality (1972). He argues that freedom (or liberty) is a basic human value that rational people in their practices would always want to include and protect and that this right to freedom will always take priority over the principle of equal opportunity. I want to develop this general position of Rawls in relation to sport and attempt to demonstrate that the practice of sport is not only a just one but essentially (despite its breakdown from time to time) a moral one.

Justice as fairness relates to sport with regard to the principle of freedom, in broad terms by an individual having the right to choose (or reject) which sport(s) to take up;[5] and in narrow terms by that individual agreeing to the rules that characterize that sport as being the particular one that it is. In so far as the individual sees his or her life and moral character bound up and coexistent with the choices he or she makes, the activities he or she enters into, the efforts he or she undergoes, the individual will see that sport is no less 'serious' and morally binding than other forms of human practice. It will be seen that although a sport may be regarded as a particular kind of practice which is characterized by its rules, it is by no means separate from or discontinuous with life or moral concern. It is in fact an identifiable form of life, and like the law or medicine, not a morally irrelevant one.[6]

Similarly, equality relates to sport in that players of a particular sport come together in the full knowledge that its rules apply to themselves as well as to others. They realize and agree that the rules that apply are in the interest of *all* players and that it is a part of the expected practice of the sport that they will be impartially applied so that one player or team will not gain unfair advantage over another. It is on this basis that sport as a competitive practice proceeds. If it was thought that the rules of sport were not concerned with the bringing about of fairness, in this sense sport would cease to be the practice it is. The player as a rational agent will not only have made a commitment about equality of treatment in advance of being a participant but as a participant will both uphold and submit to what is fair. It will be seen then, that fundamental to the concept of fairness in sport is the acknowledgement and acceptance that the rules, which both constitute and govern play, shall not only be agreed to in advance but willingly observed in practice. The point here is that both logically and morally there is only one way to play the game fairly and that is by the rules.[7]

Acting unfairly arises not so much from the accidental transgression of the rules so much as in the deliberate breaking of them. The cheat and spoil-sport are so called not because they break the rules but because they break them intentionally in the hope of gaining unfair advantage. To intentionally attempt to gain unfair advantage by breaking the rules is not to be in sport at all. It is to leave the concept and practice of sport as fair play for, as with moral duty, it implies a constraint on the doing of foul deeds to gain an unfair advantage. More than this, it recognizes the unfairness of some acts in that although they may be permitted by the rules they actually contravene the spirit of the practice.[8] Acting fairly, involves more than merely following the rules; it involves also a commitment to what they stand for in the name of what is fair. The principle of equality in sport expects the acceptance of the duty of fair play by all participants. Those who have grasped the principle will not only have adopted a common set of rules and their spirit but they will understand that it is only by practising them that the aspirations and interests of others as well as themselves can be realized. They will have seen that to recognize other players as persons, they must consider them and act towards them in certain ways. This not only leads to the preservation of sport as a practice but has clear implications for how relationships are to be conducted in terms of that practice.

In summarizing the view that sport, like some other socially constituted practices, is concerned with justice as fairness, it can be said that it is inherently concerned with the twin principles of freedom and equality. If these fundamental principles were taken away from sport, the practice as it has been constituted would cease to exist. Sport is just, in so far as all who participate in it abide by its rules and willingly submit to their binding nature and spirit, even when it is possible to gain advantage by not doing so. In many respects fair play in sport lies not so much in the hands of the referee but in the actions of players and the reasons they have for conducting themselves in the way that they do. It will thus be seen that the practice of sport as fairness and the having and forming of character are mutually supportive.

SPORT AND THE DEVELOPMENT OF MORAL CHARACTER

The character-building claims of sport are not unfamiliar. Such admired qualities as loyalty, cooperation, courage, resolution, willpower, self-control, endurance, perseverance and determination are often mentioned as arising from a participation in games and sport. It will be seen, however, that such qualities are not confined or peculiar to them. Taken on their own, however, they may be considered as desirable human traits but which are not in themselves moral. Thieves and murderers, for example, may display these same qualities and be admired for them, but nobody would wish to say that the practices they engage in are moral ones. As has been shown there is a big difference between the meaning of character in general and the development of an ethical or moral character. The conceptual question that therefore arises is this: Is sport the type of human practice that is logically tied to and consistent with the development of a moral character? If the idea of sport as fairness can be accepted, as outlined, it follows that if one is concerned with its teaching one is *ipso facto* concerned with the morality of its practice and the preservation of its ideals and standards. Sport without a proper understanding of its rules and of the underlying principles upon which those rules are based, would not be and could not be all that it is and should be in terms of moral understanding and conduct. This is a point well recognized by Aspin (1975), Meakin (1982), Fraleigh (1984) and Kretchmar (1994).

Moral character is developed in sport, as in other spheres of life, in so far as such admired human qualities as loyalty, courage and resolution are cultivated and directed to uphold what is fair and just and in the interest of all. To this extent it is being argued that the practice of sport is commensurate with moral education and the development of a moral character. Without a logical connection with morality, sport might well provide a forum for the encouragement and display of admired human virtues but it would not necessarily be in keeping with the development of moral character. To maintain that sport is a moral activity by virtue of the underlying principles, rules and ideals that characterize it, however, is not to maintain that players always and invariably act in a moral way. This they clearly do not always do.[9] The fact that this is so, however, in no way invalidates the conceptual point being made here or of its importance and implication for the sport pedagogist or the educationist in general.[10]

A further question and one which is less easy to answer is: 'Does the practice of sport demand or provide exceptional opportunities for the nurture and cultivation of admired human qualities?' In the absence of clearcut empirical evidence[11] about the relative merits of different activities in terms of moral development it is difficult to make a definitive or all-embracing judgement and yet if one looks at other forms of socially acceptable activities it is hard to escape the conclusion reached by Maraj (1965, p. 107) that: 'there are not many situations in everyday life which provide either the kind of opportunities or the number of them evoking the qualities which are considered desirable, as are provided by sport.'

What, it should be noted, is *not* being said here, is that such qualities as persistence, initiative and self-reliance are specifically and can only be trained in and through sport or that they can then automatically be transferred and applied to other spheres of life. This latter view is surely a naive and unfounded one of the relationship between sport and the development of character. Indeed it is on this point that Nisbet (1972, p. 65) observes that:

> We should not too readily jump to the conclusion that the boy who was courageous or loyal on the rugger field will automatically be courageous or loyal on the shop floor or as father of a family or (as a member) of the House of Commons.

What does seem more reasonable is the suggestion that sport, when seen and taught as a socially constituted practice concerned with fairness, provides an ethically based context of endeavour in which such qualities of character are not only encouraged but are seen to be in keeping with the best traditions of its various instances. Whilst some sports like ski-jumping place a premium on daring, coolness and self-control, others like soccer place an emphasis on cooperative effort, staying power and determination. Whereas (as far as I know), it is empirically unfounded to contend that sport or the sports field is the best training ground for the development of admired qualities of character, it does not seem at all unreasonable to suggest that sport provides an unusually good forum for the encouraged display of such qualities which are not only admired in sport but in other aspects of life. Certainly, acts of generosity and magnanimity on the sports field are universally recognized to be sportsmanlike. Similarly altruistic acts of sportsmanship such as compassion and concern are not only recognized as befitting a sportsman or sportswoman but also as being morally praiseworthy in general.[12]

It is not, as some people mistakenly imagine, the job of the physical educationist to utilize sport as a means of moral education and/or the cultivation of admired qualities of character. Rather, the physical educationist is concerned with initiating children into various kinds of physical activities, some of which are called sport. In teaching sport as a particular kind of valued human practice, however, it is the physical educationist's responsibility to see that the ethical principles upon which it is based are properly understood and that the manner in which a sport is conducted is in accord with its rules and in keeping with its best traditions. The physical educationist can guarantee nothing, but as an influential guardian of an ethically based practice he or she can do a good deal to uphold its highest ideals and its most cherished traditions. As in all forms of learning, much depends on the attitudes and judgements that are brought to bear upon what is done, and whether what is taught and encouraged is regarded as worthwhile in the context of life. As in other aspects of life, the practice of sport is an activity subject to evaluation. It can be regarded as a kind of forum for the appraisal of human conduct.

If in the past there was an all too ready assumption that attitudes and qualities encouraged and developed on the sports field were transferable into other areas of life, the present position may be regarded as confused and sceptical. It is confused because sport is still thought of by some educationists either as a morally neutral activity or in terms of play and consequently cut off from life, rather than being co-existent with it.[13] It is sceptical because there is little or no clearcut empirically based evidence to suggest a positive link between the development of admired moral qualities and a participation in sports. Observation of some forms and levels of competitive sport, as well as some empirical evidence, indeed would even suggest a negative relationship.[14] Helpful and substantiating though it would be to have proof of the effects of the 'transfer of training' arising from a participation in sport to the rest of life, it seems to me, conceptually speaking, that nothing greatly hangs upon the provision of such evidence. The fact is, the teaching of sport does and should entail the initiation of children into a form of life which because it involves the acquisition of skills, the development of practical knowledge, the active nurturing of admired human qualities, as well as moral understanding and conduct, is in effect a form of education. Put another way, an initiation into sport entails not only the acquisition and mastery of skills but the development of ethical understanding and conduct together with the cultivation of admired human virtues.

The development of a moral character in sport is best thought of in terms of a person whose actions are informed and guided by what he or she knows and understands of the rules and ethical principles upon which those rules are based, as well as by the best traditions of the practice so that fairness and self-formation result. Further, unless such virtues as courage, honesty, generosity and responsibility are practised and such vices as cheating, selfishness and brutishness avoided, the practice of sport will not be all that it can be and should be either in the development of a moral character or in the making of a contribution to the good life.

As has been indicated, the Kantian notion of 'self-formation' that can take place in sport is an important one. It goes beyond the idea of a passive compliance with the rules and acceptance of decision making and judgement by the referee. It suggests rather a rational and autonomous commitment to uphold the values of the practice and a demonstrated willingness and authenticity to abide by the rules in the interests of what is fair and just. It is by understanding that the practice of sport is essentially a moral one that the player accepts and learns to regulate his play in the interests of all. To abrogate personal responsibility for how the practice is to be conducted to the referee is an abrogation of self-command, a denial of the opportunity for self-formation. If the development of a moral character in sport means anything it is concerned with the individual player being self-governed in the sense not only of determining what he or she is going to do, but also of determining what he or she *should* do in terms of what is fair. If the idea of sport as an ethically based form of human practice is to be preserved it places considerable emphasis upon getting players to accept responsibility for what they do and act in accordance with the virtues it demands.

What then can be concluded from what has been said about sport, moral education and the development of character? It is this: that sport in common with education is inherently concerned with the moral no less than with the rational. Sport, at least in so far as it entails the promotion of moral conduct and a particular species of practical knowledge, is educative. The formation and having of character in sport, as in the rest of life, is concerned with the person in all his concrete make-up – his choices, beliefs, attitudes, feelings and behaviour. To develop a moral character does not mean the identification and cultivation of a few desirable traits which are encouraged and demanded in a number of given situations; it means rather to assist individuals towards self-formation in a principled, authentic and discerning manner, whether on or off the games field.

NOTES

1. Quote taken from Mangan (1975, p. 148).
2. Quote taken from Kitson Clark (1962, p. 271).
3. Quote taken from *Uppingham Magazine* (1972, p. 82).
4. A recent book by Shields and Bredemeier (1994) provides an excellent survey of the work done in this area. They conclude that the empirical work so far conducted on the question of whether or not sport builds character is inconclusive (p. 178). This, they think, is partially because the notion of character (as opposed to personality) has not been sufficiently clarified and partially because what has passed for character is often no more than a checklist of measurable attitudes, traits and behaviours. They point out that the sport experience is far from uniform. It not only varies from one sport to another but also in the quality of social interactions that relates to each of them. It is of interest to note that in an effort to identify what character can reasonably refer to, so that research can proceed more productively, they suggest it should be regarded as the possession of such virtues as compassion, fairness, sportspersonship and integrity. It is these qualities they maintain that are likely to facilitate the consistent display of moral action (p. 193).
   Of empirical approaches to questions of morality in general the comments by Gough (1995) should be borne in mind. That is, they should be received with circumspection because of their attempt to reduce complex matters of conduct and its interpretation of descriptive value-free data.
5. As has been intimated the matter of whether or not school games should be compulsory is an important one since it raises the question of whether or not something which is compulsory can be justified in terms of the principle of freedom. I do not propose to enter this controversy here apart from saying, along with some educationists, that it is first necessary to initiate children into an activity albeit compulsorily, before providing them with the choice of whether it is in their best interests to continue with it.
6. Two articles which are of interest here and touch upon the 'serious' and 'non-serious' aspects of play and games and have implications for sport are by Kolnai (1966, pp. 103–8) and Midgley (1974, pp. 231–53).
7. This thesis has recently been challenged. See C. K. Lehman (1981).
8. For a clear exposition of why this is so, see Fraleigh (1982, 1984).
9. For a book that summarizes some of the malpractices that go on in sport, together with some ethical issues that should be addressed in relation to them, see Lumpkin *et al.* (1994). See also Simon (1991).
10. For a helpful reminder that teachers in schools are a profession and that this entails the making of ethical judgements in relation to what one is teaching, see Shea (1978).
11. Consult Shields and Bredemeier (1994) for a useful summary of the related empirical research.
12. For an elaboration on these points see Chapter 6.
13. See, for example, Dearden (1968, 1969) and Peters (1966a).
14. See, for example, Ogilvie and Tutko (1971).

Chapter 6

Three Approaches Towards an Understanding of Sportspersonship*

A part of the tradition of sport, is the idea of sportsmanship. It is a term to which reference is often made but to which little explanation is given.[1] Even McIntosh (1979), a historian, who in his book *Fair Play* sets out 'to link an analysis of the ethics of sport with the theory and practice of education', makes only passing reference to it. Despite this neglect, however, few people would wish to deny that the relationship between sport and sportsmanship is an important one. Certainly in the games-playing ethos of the nineteenth century English Public Schools the use of one term without the other would barely have been conceivable. Today, the notion of sportsmanship continues to have social and moral implications which are relevant to and in keeping with the idea of sport as a valued human practice. It is for this reason I propose to examine the term further and attempt to clarify something of the different ways in which it has and can be used. What follows, therefore, is an attempt to help rectify what I see as a largely overlooked dimension in contemporary debate in the general area of ethics, sport and education.

Sportsmanship although most readily associated with particular types of commendatory acts done in the context of sport is sometimes extended to apply to other spheres of life and living, especially those which are concerned with competing fairly and honestly as well as with good humour. I do not propose to embark upon these latter applications but concentrate upon what I see to be its central cases, all of which are to do with the actions and conduct of sportsmen and sportswomen when engaged in sport. There are, it seems to me, essentially three different if related views about sportsmanship (or sportspersonship), each of which has implications for education, and I propose looking at each of these in turn. They are:

1. sportsmanship as a form of social union;
2. sportsmanship as a means in the promotion of pleasure;
3. sportsmanship as a form of altruism.

---

* Although I recognize the term 'sportspersonship' is a gender neutral term and is better suited to the contemporary world, it is less apposite from the historical point of view. For this reason I have decided in the present context to retain the older and more familiar term.

Before embarking upon this undertaking two preliminary comments are perhaps necessary. First, it should be made clear that although I shall be looking at each of these views separately and in turn for purposes of exposition, I do not necessarily wish to maintain that they are not to some extent overlapping or that in any one person at different times (and maybe even at the same time) all three views cannot be partially represented.

Second, it will be recalled that the idea of sport as fairness maintains that when a player enters into the institutionalized social practice of a sport he or she tacitly agrees to abide by the rules which characterize and govern it.[2] It recognizes further that if the practice of sport is to be preserved and flourish, a great deal is dependent upon the players and officials understanding and acting in accord with what is fair. They will accept and realize that breaches of the rules, especially if flagrant and deliberate, will destroy the very activity that they have agreed to participate in and uphold. They will appreciate also that if 'fairness' is interpreted too contractually or legalistically there is always the danger that that aspect of sport known as 'sportsmanship' will be construed as being only to do with those acts which demonstrate a ready acceptance of the rules and a willingness to abide by them. It will be seen, however, that this is a reasonable expectation of all players and the notion of sportsmanship connotes something more than just this. What must be underlined is that fairness, especially if understood only in a legalistic or formal rule-following sense, can only be regarded as a necessary condition of sportsmanship but by no means a sufficient one. This point applies to all three views of sportsmanship I intend to outline.

SPORTSMANSHIP AS A FORM OF SOCIAL UNION

The idea of sport as a social union takes account of but goes beyond an agreement to willingly abide by and play to the rules in the interests of what is fair. It is concerned, in addition, with the preservation and furtherance of its best traditions, customs and conventions so that the community which makes up the social union can not only cooperatively participate in sport but also successfully relate to one another as persons, through an understood, shared and appreciated mode of proceeding. It is of interest to note that 'A Sportsmanship Brotherhood' (pp. 60–1), which was founded in 1926, whilst itself was indebted to the English Public School ethos of games playing, may be regarded as a forerunner to this view. It aimed to foster and spread the spirit of sportsmanship throughout the world which it saw, in part at least, as a form of social and moral wellbeing. By adopting the slogan 'not that you won or lost – but that you played the game', it brought home the point that the manner in which sport is conducted is no less important than its outcome, if amicability and brotherhood are to be encouraged and upheld. Rawls (1973, pp. 525–6), in speaking of games as a simple instance of a social union, suggests that in addition to it being concerned with its rules it is also concerned with an agreed and cooperative 'scheme of conduct in which the excellences and enjoyments of each (player) are complementary to the good of all'.

The idea of sport as a social union, then, is not just concerned with getting players to accept and abide by the rules but with the maintenance and extolling of a way of life in which sportspersons find value, cooperation and mutual satisfaction. If this view of sportsmanship is to flourish and be furthered it is not a matter of merely adopting a particular code of etiquette or set of shibboleths, but of having a genuine commitment to the values of fellowship and goodwill which are held to be more important than the desire to win or the achievement of victory. The central purpose of the social union view of sportsmanship is to preserve and uphold fraternal relationships that can arise in and through a participation in sport. More than this, it sees this purpose as being intrinsically involved with the nature of sport itself. Any attempt, therefore, to characterize the nature of sport without reference to it would leave the concept and practice of sport incomplete and considerably impoverished. It is this point which, if properly understood by teachers, can help prevent sport degenerating, as it does from time to time, into a form of antisocial or even violent conflict.

It is important to stress that the social union view of sportsmanship is not to be seen merely as a socially cohesive device in order to help regulate and oil the institutional practice of sport, though this effect may well come about. Rather, it should be perceived as a community of individuals united by a particular practice in which the arts of chivalry are practised in the interests of mutual affection, comaraderie and fellowship. It will be seen by the participants, with the encouragement of teachers, as the kind of practice which places a high premium upon those qualities and forms of conduct such as good humour, respect, politeness and affability which are conducive to, rather than destructive of good inter-personal relations and cooperative, if competitive, endeavour. Another way to express this is to say that the idea of sport as a social union is a particular kind of social system in and by which players and officials come together in order to share a commonly valued form of life, one part of which is concerned with the manner in which one should ideally participate if the system is to flourish.[3] An example of this is provided by an incident at the French tennis championships of 1982, in which Wilander, the Swedish player, was awarded match point against his opponent Clerc on the grounds that a drive down the line was out. Wilander, instead of accepting the umpire's decision, as the rules state, asked for the point to be played again because he thought the ball was 'good and that he didn't have a chance'. Mr Dorfman, the referee, at some risk to his official position but conscious of the good of the players and game alike, agreed (Bellamy, 1982, p. 10).[4] Another example comes from the world athletic championships of 1983, when Banks, the American world triple jump record holder, was defeated in the last round by the Pole, Hoffman. Instead of being grieved and withdrawn, as is often the case when victory eludes an athlete by a hair's breadth, he demonstrated his delight at the other's success by running round the track with him for a while as an act of respect and camaraderie. For both, a momentary bond between them had been forged.

What is clear is that the system requires of all members a commitment to live out the ideals cherished by the union in a way that predisposes towards its convivial continuance. When sport is looked at in this way, sportsmanship can be seen as an evaluative term which is attributed to those who not only compete fairly in accordance with the rules but keep faith with their spirit by acts and forms of conduct which are not required by the rules but which are freely made in accord with the best traditions of competitive but friendly rivalry. This is a part of the heritage of sport into which all school children should be initiated. Conversely, antisocial acts such as riling, taunting, mocking and gloating, especially if done with malevolent intent with the idea of demeaning or underpinning the opposition and which go beyond a certain acceptable level of 'gamesmanship' would not only be regarded as bad form but bad sportsmanship and therefore something to be condemned.[5]

The social union view of sport then, apart from a ready acceptance of what is fair, sees acts of sportsmanship as being chiefly to do with the maintenance of the best traditions of sport as a valued and shared form of life. It will be seen, however, that this view of sportsmanship is more in keeping with a particular kind of socialization or ideology which predisposes group members to act in ways that are supported and admired by the social union of which they are an integral part. Because of this the social union view of sportsmanship is best understood as being more to do with an idealized form or model of group mores rather than as an individual and principled form of morality.

SPORTSMANSHIP AS A MEANS IN THE PROMOTION OF PLEASURE

The idea of sportsmanship as a means in the promotion of pleasure arises from the medieval word 'disport' which meant to distract, divert or amuse oneself. Later, especially in the social milieu of the Public Schools of nineteenth century England, it referred more specifically to outdoor games which were engaged in for the pleasure they afforded. Writing in the Contemporary Review in 1900, Graves (1900) claimed that 'sport is followed for no other end than to afford pleasure to those participating in it, and a sportsman follows sport for no other reason than to enjoy that pleasure'. Given this understanding of sport, Graves went on to suggest that sportsmanlike conduct would appear to lie in those actions that are conducive to the pleasantness of sport, and unsportsmanlike conduct to lie in these actions that spoil it by making it less pleasant.[6]

Keating's (1979) analysis of sportsmanship is in keeping with this general etymological background when he maintains that sport is 'a kind of diversion which has for its direct and immediate end, fun, pleasure and delight and which is dominated by a spirit of moderation and generosity' (p. 265). He contrasts sport with athletics which he says 'is essentially a competitive activity, which has for its end victory in the contest and which is marked by a spirit of dedication, sacrifice and intensity' (p. 265). What it is important to realize is that when Keating speaks of 'sport' and 'athletics' he does not necessarily have in mind a difference between particular activities (for example, field games and track and field) so much as an attitude or motivation towards them (1973, p. 167). With the term 'sport', he associates the notion of play and the doing of something for its own sake, and with the notion of 'athletics' he associates the notion of contest and the struggle for victory.

I do not intend to dwell upon the difficulties of holding such a simplistic either/or position. None the less, in the interests of clarity, a few brief comments seem desirable. First, whilst it may be true that play is more readily associated with some activities than with others, it should not be assumed that play is confined to them or that play can be adequately expressed only in terms of them. Play can enter 'serious' activities, like war, just as it can enter 'non-serious' ones like games. Second, the fact that an activity is 'competitive' does not necessarily preclude having a play attitude towards it. Even professional sportsmen and women can sometimes be playful. This point holds true even when recognizing that a preoccupation with winning can sometimes inhibit, even neutralize, a play spirit. To acknowledge this, however, is not to say, as Keating suggests, that if an activity is competitive it necessarily follows that a given attitude accompanies it.[7] Third, it is needlessly confusing to imply, as Keating does, that 'athletics' is concerned with competition whereas 'sport' is not. The fact is that most, if not all, physical activities commonly known as sports are competitive in one sense or another. This is a logical, if trivial, point about them. In view of this it might have been said less perplexingly that the 'sportsman's' attitude towards that family of physical activities known as sport differs from the 'athlete's'. This difference in attitude, however, stems not from the constitutive nature of the activities themselves, as Keating suggests[8] (1979, p. 266; 1973, p. 170), but rather from the way they are viewed by those who participate in them. Fourth, it does not follow either, as is suggested by some other writers,[9] that the athlete's motives are necessarily undesirable or immoral in some way. There is a big distinction, for example, between a contestant setting out to gain an honourable victory and a contestant setting out to defeat at all costs (and maybe to humiliate) an opponent.[10]

Having made these observations I wish now to examine and comment upon – accepting for the moment Keating's two ways of regarding competitive activities – what amounts to two ways of looking at sportsmanship. It would seem that for 'athletes', given their goal of 'exclusive possession' rather than cooperative endeavour, sportsmanship can never be much more than a means of taking some of the rawness out of competitive strife. Its purpose is to mitigate the effects of what is seen as a confrontation and challenge between two adversaries. Sportsmanship in these circumstances, Keating seems to be saying, can only ease, soften and in some way make more civilized, what is essentially a contest between two prize fighters. This is perhaps particularly so in sports like boxing and wrestling. The athlete will see the need for disciplined conduct and self-control, even courtesy, but he or she will not be inclined towards expressions of cordiality or generosity. Sportsmanship for the athlete, above all, means achieving victory in a dignified and honourable way. He will see the need for 'an impartial and equal following of the rules' and the need for 'modesty in victory and quiet composure in defeat'. 'Fairness or fair play', says Keating, is 'the pivotal virtue in athletics' (1973, p. 170). His chief and driving motive, however, will be the outcome of 'winning' rather than amicability or joy. In summary, Keating's presentation of sportsmanship in athletics seems pretty well commensurate with the idea of sport as justice and which, in my preliminary comments, I suggested should be an expectation of all participants. It should not perhaps therefore be regarded as a genus of sportsmanship at all. It meets minimal requirements but no more than this.

For the 'sportsman', on the other hand, sportsmanship becomes something more expansive. Here, sportsmanship is more than simply following a legislative code (which the justice theory of sport might be accused (wrongly) of being); nor is it best understood as being represented by those virtues which often accompany the admired player, such as courage, honesty, endurance, perseverance, self-control, self-reliance, sang-froid and self-respect (with which the character-development theory of sport is largely associated). Rather, it is concerned with those 'moral habits or qualities' which are essentially and characteristically to do with generosity and magnanimity (1979, p. 266). Unlike the merely 'just' player the true sportsman adopts a cavalier attitude towards his rights as permitted by the code. Instead he prefers to be magnanimous and self-sacrificing if, by such conduct, 'he contributes to the fun of the occasion' (1979, p. 266). It is important to see in Keating's account of sport that competition is not so much seen in logical terms of 'exclusive possession', by one or the other of the vying parties, but more in terms of a cooperative enterprise, which is seen to be a potentially shared source of pleasure. For Keating, then, sportsmanship for the sportsman is essentially a desirable or efficacious manner or way of acting in sport which is not only in keeping with the promotion of pleasure but is conducive to the spirit of play.

Feezell (1986), in looking at the ideas of Keating, is also troubled by his somewhat simplistic division of sport by attitude into 'play' which Keating maintains is motivated by pleasure and 'athletics' which he says is motivated by victory. In contrast to Keating, Feezell, quite rightly, I think, recognizes that the 'non-serious' and the 'serious' need not be dichotomously polarized but can exist together so that the pursuit of victory need not necessarily be at the expense of pleasure nor the pursuit of pleasure necessarily be at the expense of victory. In invoking Aristotle's notion of the mean, however, and going on to define sportsmanship as 'a mean between excessive seriousness, which misunderstands the notion of the play-spirit, and an excessive sense of playfulness, which might be called frivolity and which misunderstands the importance of victory and achievement when play is competitive', Feezell (1986, p. 10) in effect tells us little or nothing about the concept of sportsmanship. All that is being said is that good sport is, or should be, both serious and non-serious. Put differently, it suggests that sportsmanship is best understood in terms of finding a balance between the two elements which Keating chose to separate and make mutually exclusive. Now, although this approach to sport in general terms may be sensible and commendable it leaves us remarkably uninformed about those particular virtues or those forms of conduct that are being referred to when something is appraised or designated as being an act of sportsmanship. Although Feezell may have something in mind that would help clarify what he means, he regrettably provides no examples. To add to the general vagueness of his approach to sportsmanship he almost underlines it by suggesting, again following Aristotle (1985, 8094b), that like moral virtue it should be relative to us (p. 259). But surely while nobody expects absolute precision in moral matters, it is quite possible to be more objective and clear about what is to count and what is not to count as an act of sportsmanship. Without some discussion of concrete cases, we are left with the impression that it is some sort of subjective judgemental balancing act. Further, to speak, as Feezell (1986, p. 251) does, of the virtue of sportsmanship, without illustration or explication, is to suggest that the term implies a particular quality of character, like truthfulness or benevolence. This use of the definite article I think is somewhat misleading. Sportsmanship rather, I suggest, is best understood as being associated not with one virtue, but many. It manifests itself in the context of sport in a variety of acts which call upon different virtues at different times, according to the specific situation in hand. Thus, it can be exemplified, as we have seen, in terms of friendliness as well as in terms of generosity or magnanimity or again, as we shall shortly see, in terms of compassion and altruism.

From the moral point of view at least three questions arise from Keating's account of sportsmanship. The first is: Can sportsmanship in relation to sport be considered moral if it is seen only as a means or as an instrument in the promotion of pleasure?

The answer to this question is very much bound up with whether or not he is taking a utilitarian stance towards moral issues and this he does not make clear. The second question is concerned with the sense in which Keating uses the phrase sportsmanship as a 'moral category'. If he means it in the sense of being 'self-contained',[11] then it cannot properly be said to be moral since it is inapplicable to life outside sport. Similarly, if he wants to regard it as a form of play, as he seems to, then at least at one level of analysis, it is 'non-serious' as opposed to 'serious' and therefore non-moral in consequence. If, on the other hand, he is intending that sportsmanship is concerned with the type of actions that fall within the general category of the moral and therefore somehow related to the 'business of life' this should have been more explicitly stated. If this is the case, however, the problem remains as to how this interpretation is to be reconciled with the notion of play. One way round this dilemma might be to say that although play is generally regarded as a non-serious affair, this is not to say that players cannot take what they are doing seriously (in the psychological sense) or that serious incidents (e.g. death, injury or acts of malevolence) cannot occur. To say, in other words, that play as a category is non-serious and therefore non-moral, is to say that this is the way it is best understood, but recognizing, at the same time, that things occasionally occur that transform it momentarily into something else, which may or may not have moral significance.

The third question is related to the first. Even if utilitarianism is adopted as a general ethical theory it is not clear why conduct that is conducive to fun is necessarily more pleasurable and therefore more moral than conduct that is conducive to 'honourable victory'. One is tempted to ask here, whether it is not the case that the best examples of sportsmanship in terms of generosity and magnanimity arise out of the pursuit of 'honourable victory'. A case which gives some support to this thesis is when Brasher, at the Melbourne Olympic Games in 1956, was disqualified from winning the 3000 metres steeplechase for allegedly hindering his opponents. The point here is that it was these same athletes (Rosznyoi, Laresen and Loufer) who protested on Brasher's behalf and got the decision reversed, thus sacrificing the medals they would otherwise have won.

All in all, Keating's attempt to look at sportsmanship in terms of 'athletics' and 'sport' by reference to competition, or its relative absence, is conceptually confusing. Neither is it helpful from the educational point of view, especially, first, because it reduces sport to be but a means in the pursuit of pleasure and, second, in doing so, it forgoes or at least subordinates any intrinsically worthwhile claims along the lines earlier suggested. What Keating's analysis does underline, however, is the importance of the spirit that can and should be encouraged to occur in sport and the desirable attributes of magnanimity and generosity which are and should be associated with sport.

SPORTSMANSHIP AS A FORM OF ALTRUISM

It should be apparent by now that the term sportsmanship and its relation to sport and morality is a more complex and subtle one than is commonly supposed. In the social union view of sportsmanship, it was suggested that sportsmanship is largely to do with the preservation and exemplification of a valued form of life which puts a premium upon an idealized and amicable way of participating. The pleasure view of

sportsmanship is chiefly and characteristically concerned with generous and magnanimous conduct that is conducive to the promotion of fun and pleasure. The view of
sportsmanship I shall now present takes a different stance. It is concerned more with
seeing sportsmanship as a form of altruistically motivated conduct that is concerned
with the good or welfare of another. Again it should be stressed I do not see these
three views of sportsmanship as mutually exclusive. Rather I see them as providing a
different focus or perspective in a form of social phenomenon which is essentially
both recognizable and understood.

What then, more precisely, is the altruistic view of sportsmanship and how and in
what way, if at all, can it be considered as a moral form of conduct? In order to look
at the second part of the question first, I propose to contrast the Kantian view of
morality with what I shall call the altruistic view. For Kant, morality is primarily a
matter of reason and rationality. It resides in and is based upon the adoption of
principles which are universal, impartial, consistent and obligatory. It emphasizes
choice, decision, will and thoughtful deliberation.[12] Williams (1976, p. 198) in writing
of the Kantian tradition points out that:

the moral point of view is specially characterised by its impartiality and its indifference
to any particular relations to particular persons and that moral thought requires
abstraction from particular circumstances and particular characteristics of the parties,
including the agent, except in so far as these can be universal features of any morally
similar situation.

Williams continues:

the motivations of a moral agent, correspondingly, involve a rational application of
impartial principle and are thus different in kind from sorts of motivations that he might
have for treating some particular persons differently because he happened to have some
particular interest towards them (p. 198).

It will be seen that the Kantian view of morality has a lot in common with the
justice theory of sport as well as with those preconditional features of sportsmanship
which are to do with fairness. In stressing the universal and impartial, however, the
Kantian view seems to overlook or disregard some aspects of inter-personal relations
which are as morally important in sport as in other spheres of life. I refer to such
virtues as sympathy, compassion, concern and friendship. What needs to be made
clear is that the 'moral point of view', whilst importantly connected with the impartial
and obligatory, is by no means totally taken up by them. This is perhaps particularly
so in the education of the young. In speaking of sportsmanship as a form of altruism,
then, I am particularly concerned to show that sportsmanship in this sense, whilst
obligated to the following of impartial rules which govern play, at the same time gives
moral scope to go beyond them. In order to say more about this and at the same time
point up the differences between the Kantian view of morality and those aspects of
morality and sportsmanship that place greater emphasis upon the importance of
personal and particular relationships, I propose to look now at sportsmanship as a
form of altruism. At the same time I shall indicate that acts of supererogation are
more in keeping with the Kantian view than with the altruistic view.

Altruism is perhaps best understood as being to do with those forms of action and
conduct that are not done merely because of what is fair and just in terms of playing
and keeping to the rules but because, in addition, there is a genuine interest in and

concern for one's fellow competitors, whether on the same side or in opposition. At first sight it may seem as if sportsmanship in this altruistic sense is to do with supererogatory acts in that they go beyond duty or what the rules expect. In common with other forms of supererogatory acts, supererogatory acts in sport are to do, as Hare puts it, with those acts which are 'praiseworthy but not obligatory' (1981, p. 198). Put another way, to say that an act in sport is supererogatory is to say two things about it. First, the sportsman or woman is not morally (or by rule) obliged to perform it. He or she is, in other words, permitted not to perform it. Second, the action is morally praiseworthy; it would be commendable if it were performed. Urmson, in speaking of the need to make room for moral actions which lie outside the realm of the obligation, could well be speaking of the kinds of situation with which the sportsman or woman is confronted. He argues that there are a large range of actions whose moral status is insufficiently expressible in terms of the traditional classification of actions into morally impermissible, morally neutral and morally obligatory and that it is necessary to allow 'for a range of actions which are of moral value and which an agent may feel called upon to perform, but which cannot be demanded and whose omission cannot be called wrongdoing' (1958, p. 208).

There seem to be at least two ways in sport in which an act can go beyond duty (or the demands of fair play). The first way is by acting out of concern for the other or at some risk, cost or sacrifice to oneself. An example here might be the marathon runner who, at the cost of victory, stops to help a fellow runner in a state of distress. The second way is by acting on behalf of another so that more good is brought about than if one had merely acted out of duty or in accordance with the rules. An actual case of the sort of thing I have in mind here is provided by Meta Antenan, who although leading in a long jump competition against her great German rival, asked of the presiding jury that her opponent have a longer rest period than was provided by the rules, because of her having just taken part in another event (Borotra, 1978, p. 8).[13]

Such examples of sportsmanship, it might be thought, are both supererogatory and altruistic in that they go beyond what is required by duty or a proper observance of the rules, but it should be pointed out that although acts of supererogation and altruism have certain things in common – that is they have moral value and that they are not morally obligatory – they also have certain important differences which prevent one being assimilated to the other. Whereas supererogatory acts tend to stem from a traditional framework dominated by the notions of duty and obligation, and by some writers, such as Grice (1967) are even spoken of as 'ultra obligations', altruistic acts are best perceived as belonging to an entirely different realm of moral experience. Whereas supererogatory acts are seen as 'doing more than duty requires' in a sacrificial or enobling sort of way, altruistic acts are prompted by various forms of altruistic emotion. Whereas the 'supererogatory' sportsman may be prompted into acts which, to him, have the force of duty, but which he would not recognize as being incumbent on others, the 'altruistic' sportsman may be prompted into acts by the emotions of concern and care.[14]

In referring to the two examples of 'going beyond duty' forms of sportsmanship cited above, it will be seen that either or both could be considered 'supererogatory' or 'altruistic'. The correct interpretation would depend upon the considerations or states which prompted them. Moral actions in sport, like other actions, cannot be properly understood only by reference to their external form.

It will be seen then, that supererogatory or altruistic forms of sportsmanship are essentially different from those forms which are to do with a conventionalized set of values to do with preservation of amicability and group harmony or with the successful pursuit of pleasure.

What characterizes altruistic forms of sportsmanship, particularly, is that sympathy, compassion and concern are directed towards the other in virtue of his or her suffering, travail, misery or pain. The altruistic sportsman or woman not only thinks about and is affected by the plight of the other but acts in such a way that is directed to bring help or comfort in some way. Altruistic acts of sportsmanship stem from a desire for the other's good. This sometimes leads to impulsive or spontaneous forms of conduct that arise from the sporting context as when, for example, Karpati the Hungarian fencer reached out and tried to console a defeated and disappointed opponent. Such acts, it will be seen, are not motivated by such Kantian virtues as obligation and duty, so much as by a perceptive and human response to another's plight. On the rationalistic Kantian view such acts based on altruistic emotions would be considered unreliable as moral motives because they are too transitory, changeable, maybe emotionally charged and not sufficiently detached, impartial and consistent. Yet the question arises, are they less moral on account of this? Blum, who has addressed himself to this very problem argues, for instance, 'that the domain in which morally good action takes the form of universalizable principles of obligation does not exhaust the areas of morally good action' (1980, p. 93). He argues further that there are different kinds of virtues. Some are articulated by the Kantian view – justice, impartiality, conscientiousness and so on – others such as kindness, concern and compassion are articulated better by the altruistic view (1980, p. 93).

Whereas the Kantian view is predominantly concerned with what is right and what is just for all, the altruistic view is more concerned with the good of the other even if this sometimes means acting particularly and personally rather than objectively and impartially and/or in a strict accordance with what the rules decree. All in all, the altruistic view of sportsmanship, in contrast to the social union view or the pursuit of pleasure view, arises not from a concern for the preservation of a valued and particular form of inter-personal life or the promotion of pleasure as an ethic but rather from a particular and genuine concern for another's welfare. When acts in sport go beyond that which is expected of players generally and are done only out of concern for another's good and for no other reason, they are not only altruistic but exemplify the best traditions of sportsmanship. They also help characterize what it is to be morally educated.

NOTES

1. This state of affairs remains the case despite a growing number of references. See particularly: Keating (1973, 1979), Arnold (1984b), Feezell (1986) and Dixon (1992). For a useful review of the literature see Rosenburg (1993).
2. For an interesting article along these lines, see Keenan (1975, pp. 115–19).
3. This conception of the way sport can (or should) be conducted is not out of keeping with what some writers have referred to as the 'radical ethic' which recognizes that 'the excellence of the outcome is important, but holds equally important the way that excellence is achieved'. See Scott (1973, pp. 75–7). It also holds that 'the winning of the

game is subservient to the playing of the game' in which such qualities as 'corporate loyalty and respect for others' are encouraged. All in all, 'the game is viewed as a framework within which various aims may be realised, qualities fostered, needs met, and values upheld'. See Kew (1978, pp. 104–7).

4. Two points can be made about this incident. The first is that Wilander, on being asked about why he had challenged the umpire's decision, replied that he could not accept a win 'like that', by which he was taken to mean not only unfairly but in a way which would have brought dishonour to himself, and discredit from his opponent, who also thought his drive was in, as well as from fellow circuit players.

5. I recognize here as Dixon (1992) does, that the running up of a needless score need necessarily not be a case of bad sportsmanship but, if done for the wrong reasons, e.g. to humiliate the opposition, it clearly can be.

6. It is of interest to note that this etymological approach to the meaning of sport is very much in keeping with the term 'amateur' which refers to one who engages in an activity for the love of the activity itself and not for the sake of rewards that are external to it. It will be seen, therefore, as harmoniously relating to what has been said about education and sport as a valued human practice and its relationship to 'professionalism'. For a further explication of the term 'amateurism' from a historical, sociological and philosophical point of view, see the articles by Smith (1993), Harper (1993), Schneider and Butcher (1993), Morgan (1993) and Meier (1993) in volume 45 of *Quest*, 1993.

7. See Gallie (1955–6, pp. 167–98), who argued that competition is a normative concept and as such is open to being contested since the evaluative frameworks surrounding it (e.g. a 'Lombardian ethic', where winning is everything, as opposed to the 'radical ethic', referred to in note 3 above) are sometimes irreconcilable.

8. Fraleigh (1975, pp. 74–82) has touched upon some of the complexities of this issue.

9. Bailey (1975, pp. 40–50) argues that since competitive games are concerned with winning, especially when they are made compulsory, they are not only morally questionable but morally undesirable in that winning involves those behaviours and attitudes that are conducive to the defeat of the other side and all that this implies for both the winner and loser.

10. Arnold (1992, pp. 126–130) attempts to refute Bailey's view of competition and points out the difference between 'trying to win' when competing and the attitude and outcome of 'winning at all costs'. He also points out the intrinsic values of competitive games.

11. For an explication of play seen in this way, see Huizinga (1970, p. 32), Lucas (1959, p. 11) and Schmitz (1979, pp. 22–9) among others.

12. Consult Beck (1959) for a good statement of the Kantian position.

13. As a result she lost the competition by one centimetre.

14. Lyons (1983, pp. 125–45), in keeping with the points I am making, speaks about a 'morality of response and care'. This she contrasts with a 'morality of justice', which stems more from the Kantian tradition, grounded in obligation and duty. Blum (1994, pp. 247–50) also speaks of the morality of care as being particular and relational rather than universal and impartial.

Chapter 7

Sport and Moral Education

The past few chapters have been concerned with the explication of sport as a valued human practice as well as looking at its educational implications particularly with regard to such issues as competition, character development and sportspersonship. It is proposed now to relate what has been said more specifically to moral education and to the role of the teacher. In order to do this it will be helpful, first, to provide a brief overview of the way in which sport has been seen in relation to the moral life; second, to provide a background understanding of morality and how it relates to education; third, to outline what a pedagogy of sport entails with regard (a) to those processes which are basic to a moral education and (b) to those specific responsibilities the teacher should address in his or her role as educator; and fourth, to present a summary of what constitutes the morally educated person as that term applies to sport.

THREE VIEWS OF SPORT IN RELATION TO THE MORAL LIFE

A look at the place of sport in contemporary life and a study of the appropriate literature suggests that there are three broadly held views about the relationship between participation in sport (including games) and moral development. I shall refer to them as the positive view, the neutral view and the negative view. The *positive view* is the belief that there is a clear, if unproven, connection between the playing of team sports and the development of social and moral values. This belief, which emanated from the English public schools of the nineteenth century, gave birth to two theories, both of which have continued to influence attitudes towards sport, especially in its relationship to education. The first was that participation in sport, especially in the form of team games, was educationally useful in that it led to desirable social and moral outcomes. In particular, it was thought to lead to an ability to cooperate with others on a basis of understanding and mutual respect, as well as an ability to strive to the utmost in a cause without recourse to personal bitterness or vindictive meanness. In addition, it was thought that such qualities as generosity, magnanimity, courage and steadfastness could be cultivated and developed in sport. The second theory was that such training could not only be provided for on the playing fields but that its effects were transferable into the world at large and could be called upon if necessary in battle or in the service of the Empire.[1] Suffice to say that in recent years both theories have been seriously questioned. None the less, the view that sport can be used as a means of teaching social and moral values, as was indicated earlier, persists. Such sentiments are still enshrined in the movement known as Olympism, now regarded by many as outdated and antiquarian.

The second, or *neutral view*, arises from the conceptual cum classificatory position that sport is a form of play and that, because of its self-contained and separate nature, is discontinuous with the 'business of life' and is therefore, when compared to life's concerns, morally unimportant. What goes on in sport, in other words, morally speaking, is relatively inconsequential. It is essentially non-serious rather than serious. This view considers that sport, when stripped of its trappings and manufactured importance, is only a game and is not, from the moral point of view, to be compared with such matters as poverty, pestilence, war and famine. This neutralist view of the relationship between sport and morality is important not only because it has a respectable intellectual pedigree, but because it is embodied in at least one influential theory of education.[2] It does, however, I think, rest upon an inadequate understanding of sport and a too-hasty assimilation of it into the realm of play.

The third, or *negative view*, is one that largely arises from the findings of empirical studies, which are often based upon professional or high-level competitive sport where winning is deemed of crucial importance. Such studies appear to point to the fact that not only does cheating and foul play occur, but that to be successful one must possess such traits as dominance, assertiveness and non-sociability.[3] Furthermore, it would seem that the qualities often associated with sportspersonship, such as generosity and magnanimity, are more likely to be disregarded by high-level participants than by low-level ones.[4] Such findings are made abundantly apparent both on television and in the newspapers when coverage is given to big match events. Recent reviews (Shields and Bredemeier, 1994; Weiss and Bredemeier, 1986) of the empirical literature on the relationship between moral development and physical pursuits reveals a sadly ambivalent and inconclusive state of affairs. Because of the undesirable tendencies associated with some forms and levels of competitive sport, some educationists have argued (Bailey, 1975; Kohn, 1986) that competitive sport is antithetical to moral education and that it detracts from rather than enhances moral development. Such arguments about the relationship between sport and morality cannot be disregarded. On the other hand, they should not necessarily be taken as representative of the way sport is or should be conducted in general.

These three views of the relationship of sport to morality are all interwoven to some extent into the educational systems of different cultures. As a result, the picture is far from clear. It is likely to vary from one country to another,[5] even from one school to another. It is not my intention to attempt a comparative study or to comment further on these varying views, but rather to look at the relationship between sport and moral development in the context of education and to explicate what conceptual (but not necessarily factual) connections there are and what should flow from them in terms of providing guidelines for practice. I will begin by saying something about morality and moral education.

MORALITY AND MORAL EDUCATION

One important approach to morality and to moral education argues that it is concerned with the development of rational beings who are capable of making informed choices about how to conduct their lives. It suggests that individuals should take responsibility, in so far as they are able, for others as well as themselves. Such principles as justice, freedom and equality are usually acknowledged as providing the general criteria by which moral issues can be determined. They prescribe, as Peters (1981, p. 65) puts it, 'what sort of considerations count as reasons'. Arising from this approach is the ideal of a morally autonomous person who accepts or makes his or her own rules in the light of principles that he or she has chosen or adopted. What it denies is that the person has not passively assimilated them without independent scrutiny and appraisal. What it emphasizes is that the person has exercised thought and, after critical reflection, is capable of coming to a judgement. More than this, the morally autonomous person is one who is not only able to make a judgement but, by an act of will if necessary, is also able to act upon it. The moral act is not only one that is freely taken in the light of reflected upon principles, but one which is implemented if necessary with courage and determination possibly in the face of threats, bribes or social disapproval. Within this rational and principled approach then, the morally educated person is the one who not only makes moral judgements but also acts upon them. It is closely identified with Kolhberg's (1971) final stage of moral development. It is concerned with the encouragement of a capacity for moral judgement.

Two other, principles which are usually upheld as underpinning the rationality of moral discourse are those of universality and impartiality. The principle of universality, roughly speaking, upholds the view that whatever is agreed or presented as being right must apply to everyone who finds themselves in the same circumstances. The principle of impartiality emphasizes the point that whatever by way of moral prescription applies to others, also applies to me.[6] It will be seen that when an activity like sport, which is inherently concerned with justice as fairness, is freely entered into, it is necessary and expected that all who participate in it should understand and willingly abide by the rational principles upon which it is based. This is one of the key aspects of an initiation into sport, for unless this is achieved the educational justification for the inclusion of sport in the curriculum, especially from the moral point of view, is left in doubt. It is precisely because sport depends on fairness and is based upon the principles of universality and impartiality that it is not and should not be considered as a morally relative phenomenon. What I am suggesting is that cultural relativism, a descriptive thesis that recognizes certain differences between cultures (or nations), does not necessarily imply moral relativism. This is especially so when it comes to a universally valued practice such as sport. Those who have been initiated into sport know and understand that the rules that govern and characterize it apply to all. This is so whether rich or poor, black or white or from Birmingham or Bangkok. The surrounding conditions in which a sport like soccer is played may vary, but its rules and the principles upon which these rules are based remain constant. They are in fact, therefore, trans-cultural and not relative to a culture. They are the same for all peoples and all nations.

Some moral philosophers, like MacIntyre (1985), have argued that such moral principles as 'having respect for persons' or 'considering the interests of others' are so general that they present difficulties about concrete guidance. In this respect they function, as Peters (1981, p. 65) puts it, more as 'signposts than as guidebooks'. It is for this reason that other moral philosophers speak more of moral rules because they more specifically point to what moral principles entail. Thus Gert (1988, p. 284), for example, presents a moral system which meets the principles of universality and impartiality but which enjoins us to follow such specific rules as, don't kill, don't cause pain, don't disable, don't deprive of pleasure, don't deceive, keep your promises, don't cheat, obey the law, do your duty. It will be seen that these rules constitute a formidable guide to how persons ought to morally conduct themselves. They are concerned not only with self-regulation but also with inter-personal conduct. When looked at in this light it is tempting to agree with Gert (1988, p. 6) that:

> Morality is a public system applying to all rational persons governing behaviour which affects others and which has the minimisation of evil as its end, and which includes what are commonly known as the moral rules as its core.

Although Gert's moral rules have the merit of being clear, they can be criticized on the grounds that they place the emphasis on negative conduct rather than on encouraging people to follow such positive injunctions as be truthful, be trustworthy, be fair, be honest or be dependable. In the context of education, it seems to me important that positive qualities should be praised no less than antisocial forms of behaviour condemned. What perhaps is not always sufficiently recognized in relation to a practice like sport is that every violation of a moral rule (e.g. those concerned with the prevention of injury) frequently leads to two negative but related consequences. First, it tends to weaken the agent's tendency to act in accordance with the rule and thereby to jeopardize the agent's prospect of achieving moral worth. Second, the violation of a moral rule (e.g. intentionally causing injury to another player) undermines the idea of a valued practice and, in consequence, introduces into it an element of instability and mistrust.

As was intimated earlier, to subscribe to a set of rules is one thing, but to act upon them when perhaps one feels disinclined is another. Many writers, therefore, insist that the will is an important element in moral conduct. If one is able to see what one ought to do in a given situation and yet not act upon it, one leaves what is required unfulfilled. The moral agent in contrast will act despite, perhaps, a disinclination because he or she will feel obliged to do so, and will be acting out of duty and a sense of what is right. The 'goodwill' according to Kant (1959, p. 10) is good not because of what it did or did not bring about but because of its intent. The goodwill he explains is not a mere wish but 'the summoning of all the means in our power to do the deed which is our duty'. It will be seen then, that the moral person is one who not only recognizes a moral situation and what principles and rules apply to it, but will act in accord with what is required, regardless of any inclination not to do so. What has been said applies to people in sport no less than to those who engage in other aspects of life. Sport is not, as some writers think play is, removed from the real world and, therefore, free of moral prescription. Rather, like the practices of medicine or engineering, it is a part of the social fabric of community life. An attempt to injure or maim in sport, therefore, is no less an offence against another person because it was done on the playing field rather than off it.

Apart from principles and rules it is possible to say something more about the moral life by reference to the virtues. Aristotle (1973) thought that the virtues could be divided into two forms – intellectual and moral. The former is concerned with the pursuit and establishment of theoretical knowledge for its own sake. The latter is concerned with the ability to do the right thing in practice. Both, Aristotle argued, are necessary to the good life of man, which was to live well. Both, it will be seen, have implications for education. Here, however, I shall be mainly concerned with practice.

Our character, Aristotle argued, is made up of the virtues it comes to have by exercising them. Character is not something with which we are born. It is something which is learned by habit or regularly acting in a particular way. A virtue such as courage, for example, is developed by acting courageously. One learns the virtue of justice by being just; of truthfulness by truth telling; of temperance by being temperate. Aristotle argues not only that the virtues are acquired by practise but that they constitute states of character.

For an action of a person to be morally virtuous, Aristotle argues, it must fulfil at least three conditions. First, it should be controlled by reason; a person should know and understand what he or she is doing. Second, it should follow the principle of the mean. In the case of courage, for example, an act should neither be foolhardy or reckless nor cowardly or timid. It should be neither of these extremes, which are vices, but something nearer the middle. Third, it should be deliberately chosen, neither forced nor an accident. Unlike Kant's virtuous person who does things out of duty, Aristotle's virtuous person does them without difficulty because, by upbringing and training, he or she does them as a matter of course. When Aristotle speaks of excellence of character, he is referring to a settled disposition to act with reason in a way that is appropriate to the situation.[7] Thus, in terms of an academic pursuit like history, one would act in a scholarly way by being thorough, diligent, truthful, imaginative, clear and coherent. Similarly, in a practical pursuit like rugby a different set of virtues which are appropriate to pursuing this activity well would come into play. Thus such qualities as fairness, honesty, courage, determination, generosity and fellowship would be practised and habituated because these are the ones that the ethos of the activity demands. This is necessary and desirable because without them sport is not all that it can and should be, both in terms of itself and human development and wellbeing.

What should be understood about the morality of virtue is that human excellences or virtues such as justice, friendliness and tolerance should not only be pursued for their own sake – that is in terms of their intrinsic human worth – but also because they are a necessary part of those activities which are valued. What might be called the personal and public aspects of life are inextricably linked. Only if the virtues flourish both at an individual and institutional level can a person's wellbeing and that of the community be achieved. Put another way, the morality of virtue entails that the virtues should not only have intrinsic worth in terms of an individual's personal development but have functional or objective worth in the sense that they have an impact upon the activities and business of everyday life.

When looked at from the perspective of the moral virtues, moral education lies in the attempt to develop human excellences such as honesty, truthfulness and courage in such a way that they are informed by reason and dispose towards right conduct that is appropriate to a given situation or activity. Thus, it can be said that a morally educated person has a willing disposition to act appropriately in accordance with reason and virtue.

It should not be thought, in view of what has been said, that moral education is only concerned with the making of moral judgements and having the will and capacity to act upon them. Clearly, other considerations are also important. Wilson (1971), for example, in addition to the cognitive, and volitional aspects of moral education also recognizes that the affective dimension has its part to play. To enable children to see that the feelings of other people count as much as their own, and an ability to empathize with other people in various sorts of situations, are as much a part of being morally educated as being able to think and to act in a principled or rule-governed way. Blake touches upon this compassionate side of moral education when he asks:

> Can I see another's woe
> And not be in sorrow too?
> Can I see another's grief
> And not seek for kind relief?
> (William Blake, 'On Another's Sorrow')

It is in an effort to recognize the legitimacy of the above questions and sentiments in the context of the prevailing morality of justice with its emphasis on principles and rules, that some contemporary moral educationists, such as Gilligan (1982) and Noddings (1984), bring to our attention those aspects of a personal relationship that are concerned with caring. This is perhaps particularly important in the upbringing of young children, where they not only need to be 'habitualized' before they can think for themselves into considerate and acceptable forms of conduct, but given the concern and affection that is their due. It should not, however, be thought that reason and habit or reason and compassion, are opposites and have no common ground or purpose. Peters (1972) clearly sees this when he observes that the unity of moral life involves not only the rational pursuit of the good but is involved also with a concern and love for particular others.

Pring (1984, p. 117), in seeing moral education as a part of personal and social development, advocates a form of curriculum which takes account of at least four factors. First, cognitive capacity, which includes the developing capacity to think in terms of fairness and in terms of principles. Second, the facts to be known, which, in the case of sport, would involve knowing the rules. Third, a bundle of interrelated considerations, which he labels attitudes, feelings and dispositions. This would include, in the case of sport, the generation of an appropriate attitude towards the rules and the referee, as well as a respect for and empathy towards one's fellow players. Fourth, practical application. This, again in the case of sport, involves the concrete living out of the previous three factors. To do this takes 'strength of character', especially if what is seen to be 'right', goes against prevailing group pressure or mores.

In speaking then of principles, rules, virtues, the morality of caring and personal and social development, I have attempted to bring together what is centrally involved in being moral and what its implications are for education. The task now is to relate some of the points that have been raised to the teaching of sport when seen as a valued human practice. Much of this is implicit in what has gone before. What follows should be seen as a final endeavour to both summarize and give guidance about what the teacher of sport can reasonably be expected to do when looked at from the point of view of his or her moral responsibilities.

PEDAGOGIC PERSPECTIVES

Earlier, sport as fairness was discussed as if all players, whether adult or children, are rational and will conduct themselves on the field in accordance with rules which have an underlying ethical basis. It is of course unlikely that sport will ever be practised universally in the way it should be. Too many chauvinistic, socio-economic pressures or prestige factors militate against this. None the less, from the pedagogic point of view it is necessary to attempt what ought to be the case. In this connection it is proposed to say something about the idea of initiation into sport before going on to outline the general perspectives of moral education, the role of the teacher and the moral outcomes of a successful initiation into sport as a valued human practice with particular reference to fairness, the development of character and the cultivation of sportspersonship.

Initiation into Sport

Unless children are systematically brought to understand the nature of the practice of sport, and the principles upon which it is based, it cannot be said they have been properly initiated into it. This, as Arnold (1992) has shown, not only requires an understanding of the rules of sport, but an understanding of its skills, standards and excellences as well as its traditions, customs and conventions.

It requires too, an understanding that sport as a valued human practice is characterized by a moral ethos which is dependent upon, and linked to, the exercise by its participants of such virtues as honesty, fairness and courage. Another way of putting this is to say that an initiation into the ideal of sport requires that its participants possess those virtues that are both necessary to its characterization as well as to its successful practice.

It should be realized, however, that understanding alone, even if it is at a post-conventional, autonomous and principled level – the highest of Kohlberg's (1971) stages of moral development – will not necessarily generate conduct in accordance with what is understood. As is well known, right reasoning in moral matters is not always accompanied by right conduct. Acting rightly in sport (as elsewhere) is as much a matter of caring and motivation as it is of reasoning; and unless teachers can engender through their own attitudes, beliefs and dispositions, a sense of what is understood as mattering in terms of what is practised, there is little prospect that moral education in any full sense of that term will occur. It is important, therefore, that teachers practise what they do with skill and commitment as well as with knowledge and understanding. Accomplishing this means combating in a deliberate and planned way the Lombardian view that winning is the only thing that matters, and replacing this view with a clear conception of what constitutes 'the good contest'. Fraleigh (1984), in speaking of 'right actions' in this context, refers to such guides as non-injurious action, mutual respect and sympathetic regard, all of which are in keeping with the idea of moral education. Similarly, Keating (1988) and Arnold (1984b), in discussing the notion of sportspersonship, point to the manner in which sport should be conducted if a knowledge of and commitment to the rules of sport are to be transformed from legalistic precepts into real inter-personal, social and moral experience. A practical corollary to this is that the teaching and learning of 'professional fouls', which are committed to overcome a threatening situation or gain a tactical advantage (that some teachers/coaches uphold as legitimate) and which incur known and predictable outcomes, should be condemned as offending the spirit of the rules and the principles upon which they are based.

Moral Dimensions of an Education in Sport

Underlying and consistent with what has been said so far about morality and moral education and an initiation into sport, is the fact that much depends upon the interlocking processes of judging, caring and acting. It is these processes according to Hersh *et al.* (1980) that constitute the basis of moral education.

In the context of a sport as a valued human practice *judging* is concerned with what is 'right' or 'wrong' about an action first, in terms of its rules and the ethical principles upon which they are based, and second in terms of its best traditions, customs and conventions. These guidelines provide the criteria for acceptable conduct. They form the intellectual or rational bed-rock upon which decisions are or should be made. Moral judging in sport, as in other spheres of life, requires the ability to evaluate conflicting interests in the light of recognized criteria.

Caring in sport involves more than a concern for the preservation of sport as a valued human practice in some abstract sense but a concern about the manner in which sport should be conducted at an inter-personal level. It entails a whole range of emotions, feelings and sentiments that are concerned with the interests and needs of all participants, both on and off the field of play. Caring involves an ability to perceive another in a particular way – as a person with whom one is in relation, whether as comrade or competitor, in a shared enterprise mutually agreed upon. Caring involves the emotions – a capacity to feel for or empathize with the state of another. At the heart of caring is a concern for the welfare of one's fellow participants and a disposition to act towards them in a benevolent way.

Without the third process of *acting*, moral education in sport would be left incomplete. Important though the processes of judging and caring are, they are left unfulfilled unless they are realized in the taking of an appropriate action. The ideal moral act is one that is based upon rational thought, appropriate feelings and relevant action. In sport, this can only be appraised in terms of it being viewed as a valued human practice, and a comprehensive understanding of what this entails by way of actions that are not only prescribed and proscribed by the rules but in keeping with its highest standards and traditions. Moral actions in sport, as with moral acts in other spheres of life, are to an important degree intentional, voluntarily entered into and concerned with the welfare of oneself and others. A person properly initiated into the practice of sport will, for the most part, know how to respond to the question 'What should I do?' He or she will, as was made clear earlier, be concerned more with the intrinsic values and demands of the activity rather than its extrinsic pressures or rewards. He or she will be as much concerned with the moral manner in which something is achieved as in the achievement itself.

What should perhaps be emphasized is that to act morally in sport is not simply to *follow* the rules in an uninformed way, like a well-programmed robot, but to *act* in accordance with them in an enlightened way so that the interests of the practice and all its participants can be realized.

The Role of the Teacher

It is sometimes said that every teacher is a 'moral educator', but this is occasionally challenged on the grounds that not all teachers are trained or competent in moral matters, and that, even if they were, being in a position of authority in some ways militates against acting as a moral educator. It is not proposed to debate either of these issues here. Instead I will start from the premise that both these points do not apply and take the view that the teacher can and should, directly or indirectly, have a moral influence upon the pupils with whom he or she comes in contact and that the role of the teacher *per se* does not unduly inhibit, if it inhibits at all, the process of moral education. The question then that will be addressed here is, What can the teacher of sport reasonably do in order to promote moral education?

There are at least three things that can and should be done in order to assist moral growth. These are concerned with the role of the teacher as an initiator into and guardian of the practice view of sport; as an enlightened leader of discussion; and as the provider of individual pastoral care. Each will be discussed briefly in turn. The role of the teacher as exemplar will also be considered.

The Teacher as an Initiator into and as a Guardian of the Practice View of Sport

Any pupil being initiated into a particular sport will be expected to learn the rules that govern and characterize that activity, but it is the responsibility of the teacher to explain that at heart they are to do with fairness and having a respect for all of the participants, whether on the same side or in opposition. Views that may be expressed or enacted concerned with cheating, dangerous play or unacceptable behaviour should not be condoned but condemned, not only because they offend the rules of the activity but also its spirit. Conversely, acts of consideration or sportspersonship, although not required by the rules, should be recognized and commended as in keeping with sport as a valued practice. Just as attention should be paid to the rules of sport and the ethical principles upon which they are based, as well as to its skills, techniques, tactics and strategies, so too should attention be paid to its moral ethos and the ideals and virtues in which it is rooted.

It is in all these respects that the teacher will act as guardian, guide and mentor. It is by caring about sport as a practice and making informed judgements in relation to it that the teacher will pave the way to an understanding of sport and the manner in which it should be conducted, if its finest conventions and traditions are to be upheld.

The Teacher as an Enlightened Leader of Discussion

It is inevitable that situations arise in sport that both require and provide opportunities for comment and discussion. These might emerge from the playing of a game
and can be quickly settled by a reference to the rules. There may be other more
general matters, however, that require considerable knowledge and understanding if
they are to be considered in a rational and sensitive way. I have in mind here such
issues as winning at all costs, the use of 'professional' fouls, the taking of performance-
enhancing drugs, as well as such social concerns as race, gender, commerce and
politics in relation to sport. All these topics may seem a long way removed from the
practice view of sport, yet it should be realized, not least by pupils in school, that
modern sport, especially at representative level, is bound up with them. It is,
therefore, necessary for the teacher to have at least an acquaintance with the place of
sport in society and confront the problems that this can pose for sport as a form of
education within the school. The teacher can confront these both formally, in the
form of structured lessons in which points of view are expressed, as well as informally
in his or her day to day observations and the attitudes these may foster.

Although teachers in their formal position of authority are expected to be rational
and objective in the presentation of arguments, this does not necessarily mean that
they must remain silent about which particular view they personally hold. On the
contrary, it seems to me important and desirable that they reveal their viewpoint and
integrity if they are to be respected. As Warnock (1977, p. 143) puts it: if the teacher
as a moral agent is to affect the moral development of others, he must show that he
has 'views, principles, attitudes – even passions' himself.

The Teacher as a Provider of Individual Pastoral Care

No matter how clear the message is about what conduct is appropriate to the practice
view of sport, there will be those who know what is 'right' but do what is 'wrong'.
There is an inconsistency between what they know and understand and how they
conduct themselves. There, of course, may be many reasons for this disparity between
thought and action. It may be a failure of know-how or of caring. Whatever the
explanation it becomes, in the first instance at least, it is the responsibility of the
teacher to provide some individual counselling. This will inform and bring home to
pupils that conduct in sport, as in other walks of life, is not a matter of indifference
but of concern because it affects others as well as themselves. This is so, it should be
pointed out, whether it relates to a deliberate transgression of the rules governing
procedures or whether it relates to the intentional injury of another. The practice
view of sport, it should be explained, is dependent upon mutual cooperation and
respect in the interests of what is fair. To undermine sport by flouting its rules and
conventions is to corrupt and spoil it as a worthwhile pursuit. If after counselling,
miscreant behaviour continues, then the issue arises as to whether the individual
should be permitted to continue as a participant.

The Teacher as Exemplar of the Values Embodied in Sport

It has been suggested that moral education in sport, as in other spheres of life, is concerned with the processes of judging, caring and acting in relation to a concern for the interests and welfare of others as well as ourselves. Much of this aspect of education, as has been outlined, can and must in the case of sport be directly taught but a lot also depends upon the individual teacher and the ideals and values he or she both embodies and projects. In matters of moral development this is particularly important for no matter what teachers may formally do as a result of the position they occupy, it will count for little unless, by example, they live out the values to which they are committed and publicly extol. It is not without reason that it has been said of moral education that it is as much 'caught' as 'taught'. Whether the sports' teacher likes it or not, his or her thoughts, feelings and dispositions are 'picked up' and become, for better or worse, a model of what is normal or even acceptable. As has already been intimated, rationality and knowledge 'about' what is required in moral matters does not always lead to appropriate feelings or right actions. In moral matters they stand a better chance of doing so if they are seen to come shiningly together in the case of influential others. In this respect the teacher and the parent are crucial figures. On this point Carr (1991, p. 258) comments that:

> A good teacher is not just the technically efficient deliverer of certain curricular goods. He or she is the kind of person who is looked up to by virtue of possessing certain admirable qualities of character upon which it is appropriate to model our lives.

What is important is that the teacher of sport be the kind of person who not only cares about the worthwhileness of what is being taught, but teaches it in such a way that such qualities as fairness, consideration, courage, honesty and compassion are in evidence. As suggested earlier, if what it is to be moral is to be conveyed indirectly as well as directly, it had best be done in an unobtrusive way by somebody who is authentically moral and possesses the qualities that are occasionally extolled and which are a necessary part of the practice called sport.

FAIRNESS, CHARACTER AND SPORTSPERSONSHIP: THREE MORAL MANIFESTATIONS OF A SUCCESSFUL INITIATION INTO SPORT

It has been argued that sport, when understood as a valued human practice, is inherently concerned with the moral and that to be successfully initiated into it is necessarily a part of moral education. To think otherwise is to misunderstand the nature of the practice. This, of course, is not to say that an initiation into sport inevitably brings successful results. Clearly it does not. This is manifestly evident from the way sport is sometimes played. The point of this final section is not to debate what are often the facts of the matter, but to present an outline of what is logically entailed when a successful initiation into sport does take place. At the risk of some repetition, this will be done with particular reference to the exemplification of fairness, development of moral character and to the cultivation of sportspersonship.

The Exemplification of Fairness

It was suggested earlier that the idea of justice as fairness, as explicated by Rawls (1972), relates to sport, with regard to the principle of freedom, by an individual having the right to choose or reject a certain sport.[8] In narrow terms, it relates to his or her agreeing to the rules characterizing that sport. In so far as the individual sees his or her life and moral character bound up and coexistent with his or her choices, activities and efforts, that person will see and understand that sport is no less serious than other forms of human practice. The point here is that, although a sport may be regarded as a particular kind of practice characterized by its rules, it is by no means separate from or discontinuous with life or moral concern. It is, in fact, an identifiable form of life and like other valued practices such as the law is not a morally irrelevant one.[9]

Likewise, the principle of equality relates to fairness in sport in that players of a particular sport come together in the full knowledge that its rules apply to themselves as well as others. They understand that the rules are in the interest of all participants and are expected to be applied impartially so that one player or team will not gain an unfair advantage over another. It is on this basis that sport as a competitive practice does or should proceed. Contestants agree that, both logically and morally, there is only one way to play the game fairly – and that is by the rules.[10] They realize that acting unfairly arises not so much from an accidental transgression of the rules as in the deliberate breaking of them. The cheat and spoil-sport are so called not because they break the rules, but because they break them intentionally to gain an unfair advantage. To intentionally attempt to gain unfair advantage by breaking the rules is not to be *in* sport at all. It is to turn away from the concept and practice of sport as fair play for, as with moral duty, sport implies a constraint on the doing of foul deeds to gain an unfair advantage. Furthermore, the true sportsperson will see that some acts, although permitted by the rules, may actually contravene the spirit of the practice.[11]

The principle of equality, then, expects the duty of fair play to be accepted by all participants. Those who live out the principle will not only have adopted a common set of rules and their spirit, but will also understand that it is only by practising the rules that the aspirations and interests of others, as well as their own, can be realized. They will know that to recognize another player as a person one must consider and act towards that player in certain ways. This not only helps preserve sport as a practice but has clear moral implications for how relationships are to be conducted in terms of that practice.

The Development of Moral Character

It was mentioned earlier that in the view of Kant (1991) the primary end of education is the development of moral character. Whilst some contemporary educationists may question its prioritized status, few would question that it is a matter of central concern. However, before discussing how sport can assist in this process, let us once more be clear what features and qualities of a person's make-up are being referred to when he or she can be said to have a moral character.

It suggests first of all that the person is rational and makes choices and performs actions that are in accordance with such principles as impartiality and universality which helps identify what it is to be moral. It suggests also, that once a set of values and principles have been established and a commitment made to them, that they should be lived out with integrity and consistency. Having a moral character, then, is to be rationally autonomous and to act in accordance with what this dictates. It is to do, as Peters (1966b, p. 265) expressed it, with what a person 'decides to be' in the interests of what is moral. It suggests that part of a person's make-up is self-regulatory and self-determining. It suggests, in some situations an exercise of reason over habit; control over inclination; duty over prudentiality; strength of will over weakness. Above all, to have a moral character is to suggest that a person is able to act responsibly in relation to himself and others in the different contexts in which he finds himself. To say a person has moral character is to praise that person. It is to say of that person that he or she is generally considered good, rather than bad.

Another way of speaking of the person who has moral character is to say that he or she possesses certain moral virtues. Aristotle (1973) it will be recalled, suggests that the idea of a virtue represents a kind of human excellence which helps bring harmony and cooperation within a community as well as within the different practices of which it is largely comprised. A virtue for Aristotle, it will be remembered, is 'a state of character' and concern with the exercise of rational choice. In so far as such virtues as fairness, honesty, trustworthiness and dependability are concerned with character development, they become a part of moral education. Such virtues are moral because they constitute the very qualities by which a person's conduct is morally appraised both within and across the different contexts of his or her life. They help provide the criteria by which moral judgements are made. Furthermore, as MacIntyre (1985, p. 187), has emphasized, virtues are more than just admirable traits of character. They are cardinal features of what he calls a 'practice'. They presuppose a set of ideals, a sense of what people are meant to strive for and admire. They constitute the essence of what it is to have an ethos.

What then, more specifically, is it to have a moral character in the context of sport as a valued human practice? It lies, having been initiated into it, in making a commitment to its internal goals and standards. This entails acting in accordance with its rules and upholding its best customs, conventions and traditions. It involves exercising those virtues such as honesty, fairness, courage, determination and persistence which not only help characterize sport as a practice, but which are indispensable elements in allowing it to flourish.

It can be said then, that there is a reciprocal relationship between sport and moral character. Sport both needs participants who have moral character in order to survive the external social, economic and political pressures that impinge upon it and, at the same time, has the possibility of developing character by calling upon those virtues such as honesty that are an inherent part of what the practice demands. The development of a moral character in sport as a part of the educational process does not occur so much as a result of using sport in an instrumental way but rather in the pursuit of sport for its own sake.

What is not being maintained here is that such qualities as fairness, honesty, courage and so on are peculiar to sport or can only be developed in or through sport.

Clearly, this is not the case. The claim of sport in the development of a moral character lies rather in the fact that there are not many activities in life that provide a logical connection with morality as well as actually calling upon and extolling those qualities that are considered desirable.

The Cultivation of Sportspersonship

The manifestation of a moral character in sport is often depicted in terms of a willing submission to the rules and obligations of sport as a valued practice. This, of course, is no more than it should be but the possibilities for a moral education in sport do not end here. There is also the question of sportspersonship. This goes beyond a proper appreciation of the rules in terms of what is fair. It is concerned rather with certain types of commendatory acts done in sport which are not obligatory but which enrich it as a worthwhile practice. It is for this reason, it is sometimes said, that sport without sportspersonship would leave it considerably impoverished. Its rules would remain but its ethos would diminish. Another way of understanding sportspersonship is to see it as being concerned with the exercise of such virtues as friendliness, generosity and compassion in the conduct of sport. It is by reference to these three virtues that I now propose to outline what earlier I called the three views of sportsmanship. I shall refer to them as the social union view, the magnanimity view and the altruistic view. It should be noted that although each of them highlights a particular virtue together with its related constellation of qualities and dispositions, they are not mutually exclusive. They each to an extent overlap one with the other. It should be understood also that, as with all actions, acts of sportspersonship can only be fully appreciated or judged when seen against the background of a person's intentions and motivations within a particular context.

The *social union view* places a premium upon the idea of fellowship and amicability and the manner in which sport is conducted. It sees sport as the kind of practice that is not only concerned with a willing acceptance of the rules, but with the extolling of a way of life in which honour, respect, politeness and friendliness are made manifest because it is thought they are conducive to good inter-personal relations among and between participants. Sportspersonship, according to this view, is seen as being to do with those acts of cooperation that are to do with conviviality and social harmony. It not only acts as a social lubricant but brings about a mutual trust and respect among sportsmen and sportswomen.

The *magnanimity view* of sportspersonship is concerned with the virtue of generosity. It is this quality for Keating (1988) that characterizes the central meaning of sportspersonship. He writes: 'The sportsman is not in search of legal justice; he prefers to be generous whenever generosity will contribute to the fun of the occasion.' Generosity as a trait of character and as a virtue characteristic of sport, is best understood as an act that is neither legally nor morally required of a participant but which, none the less, is carried out and seen by others as praiseworthy and in keeping with the ethos of the practice. In tennis the acknowledging of a good shot by an opponent or offering to replay a disputed line call are examples of generous-mindedness in action. The point then about generosity as a manifestation of sportspersonship is that it is not obligatory. On the contrary, it is freely given. It is a mark of goodwill towards the recipient and, at the same time, serves as an example of the manner in which the practice of sport should be conducted.

A third, the *altruistic view* of sportspersonship, which can be seen as an aspect of moral education, is concerned with those forms of conduct which are directed towards the good or welfare of another. Altruism may best be seen as being related to what was said earlier about benevolence and caring.

It should be noted that in contrast to the Kantian (1991) and Kohlbergian (1971) views of morality, which are essentially to do with justice as fairness, the altruistic view of sportspersonship, stresses not so much the rules and their implications for an activity, but such complementary virtues as sympathy, compassion and concern for the stress or plight of another. In a sense altruistic acts of sportspersonship are superegogatory acts. That is to say they, like acts of friendliness and generosity, are praiseworthy but not obligatory. It is quite permissible not to perform them but they are acclaimed when they are. They may be compared almost to those acts in the Christian tradition that are deemed 'saintly'. An example here might be the case of a cross-country skier who, at some cost to himself, stops to help at the collapse and distress of another. The point about such acts is that they stem from a desire to assist, or comfort in some way, perhaps at some sacrifice to oneself. They may also sometimes be spontaneous and less sacrificial, as when one athlete may reach out to provide consolation at the disappointment of another.

Such acts are not motivated by such rationalistic principles as duty and obligation so much as by a perceptive and compassionate response to the needs of another. On a Kantian view of morality altruistic acts of sportspersonship are considered unreliable as moral motives because they are too transitory, changeable and emotionally charged and not sufficiently detached, impartial and consistent. Yet are they less moral on account of this? Blum (1980), and more recently Gilligan (1982) and Noddings (1984), think not. They argue that such principles as universality and impartiality do not exhaust the areas of morally good actions and that there are different kinds of virtues. Some are articulated by the Kantian view – justice, duty and conscientiousness and so on – while others, such as kindness, concern and compassion, are articulated better by the altruistic view. What should be understood from this is that both views are valid aspects of a moral education and are relevant to the manner in which sport as a valued human practice should be conducted.

SUMMARY

Overall, what has been shown is that sport, when seen as a valued practice, is inherently concerned with the moral. It is as a result of being properly initiated into sport that the processes of judging, caring and acting become operative and manifest themselves in terms of fairness, the development of moral character and sportspersonship. In this the teacher's role as educator is of cardinal importance. Sport in education should not be conceived as being *used* for moral purposes, but rather as a worthwhile practice in which the principles that underlie it and the virtues that are both necessary to it and help characterize it have a necessary and vital part to play in the emergence of a morally educated person.

NOTES

1. For further comment on these points, see McIntosh (1979).
2. See Peters (1966a) and Dearden (1968, 1969).
3. One of the best-known attacks on the assumption that sport builds character. See Ogilvie and Tutko (1971).
4. For a helpful summary of the effects of sport on the reduction of pro-social tendencies, see Kleiber and Roberts (1981, pp. 115–16).
5. There is some evidence to suggest that cheating, at least at the university level of sport, is culture-specific. See Jones and Pooley (1982, pp. 19–22).
6. For a more detailed treatment of the relationship between universality and impartiality see Hare (1981).
7. Urmson (1988, p. 28) notes that what is appropriate must be explained by reason; excellence of character can merely ensure willing compliance with the requirements of practical thinking.
8. The matter of whether school games should be compulsory is important because it raises the question of whether something compulsory can be justified in terms of the principle of freedom. Here I will only say, along with some educators, that it is first necessary to initiate children into an activity, albeit compulsorily, before letting them choose whether it is in their best interests to continue with it. For further comment on this point and related ones, see Arnold (1988).
9. Two articles of interest here that touch upon the serious and non-serious aspects of play and games and have implications for sport are by Kolnai (1965–6, pp. 103–8) and Midgley (1974, pp. 231–53).
10. This thesis has recently been challenged. See Lehman (1981).
11. For a clear exposition of why this is so, see Fraleigh (1982).

Chapter 8

Sport, Democracy and Education

The preceding chapters have been predominantly concerned with the explication of sport as a valued human practice and how this relates to educational issues and concerns. They have attempted to demonstrate that when sport is seen and understood as a practice it is necessarily moral in nature and that it contains inbuilt guidelines for how it should be conducted. They provide an evaluative framework by which actions in sport can be judged as being appropriate or inappropriate, moral or immoral. Chapter 7 in particular summarizes the case of sport as a distinctive and contributory part of moral education. The purpose of this final chapter is, first, to explicate the place of sport in a liberal education and what importance this can have on the development of what it is to be a person, and second, to demonstrate that the social principles of freedom and equality not only underlie the notions of sport as fairness but are at the heart of the educational process and what it means to live in a democratic society.

I shall start by looking at the meaning of democracy, then go on to outline what I mean by a liberal education and show how the democratic ideal is dependent upon it. Lastly I shall argue that sport not only instantiates a part of what it is to be educated but that in a democratic society the possibilities it offers for personal development should be a matter of social provision and made a part of governmental policy.

THE MEANING OF DEMOCRACY

The term democracy has been dismissed as 'notoriously useless' yet it remains one which is important. It probably originated in the fifth century BC as the name given to a system of government to be found among the Greek city–states. It referred to rule 'by' or 'of' the people. Democracies were regimes in which citizenship, or the possession of a right to participate in public affairs, was widely shared among 'the many'. At the time democracies were contrasted with rule by the few (oligarchy), the nobility (aristocracy), the one (monarchy) and an unconstitutional dictator (tyranny).

What characterized democracy was the right of all to decide what were matters of general concern.

Much of what is meant by democracy today can be conveyed in three phrases. The first, *by-the-people*, provides a criterion by which the institutions and procedures of government can be checked upon to see whether or not they embody and express the will of those governed. The second phrase, *for-the-people*, provides a criterion to examine whether or not those in office are in fact making decisions, passing laws and voting effectively and in the best interests of the people as a whole. The third phrase, *of-the-people* provides a criterion to see whether or not both in government, and in other institutions, recruits are being drawn from persons of every kind of social background.

What is clear, although it was not always the case,[1] is that today democracy is a term of approval, and that despite the many political and social contexts in which the term is used, to say that an idea or an institution is democratic is to implicitly commend it. Can some features be pointed to over and above those already outlined that would help test and verify whether or not government (or some other institution such as the law or education) is democratic? The following questions are perhaps helpful. Are elections free and held periodically? Has every citizen the right to vote? Are parties and candidates entitled to stand in opposition to those in office? Is the voter protected against intimidation by the secrecy of the ballot? Does a majority vote against the party in power lead to a change of government? Has the elected body the right to vote taxes and control the budget, deciding such matters, if necessary, by majority vote? Does the elected body have the right to publicly question, discuss, criticize and oppose government measures without being subject to threats of interference or arrest?

What emerges from such features, posed in the form of questions, is that democracy is based on the belief that each human being is of value; and that each citizen is guaranteed certain rights that operate in practice and are not just formal. These include such human rights as security against arbitrary arrest and imprisonment; freedom of speech, of the press, television and other forms of media, as well as of assembly; freedom of petition and association (i.e. the right to form parties, trade unions and other societies); freedom of movement; freedom of religion and teaching. A corollary of democracy, as Bullock (1977, p. 161) points out, is the establishment of an independent judiciary and courts to which everyone can have access.

If this somewhat sketchy picture of democracy can be accepted as being reasonably representative of its meaning, it will be seen that two general social principles underpin it: those of freedom and equality. Freedom is important because it allows the views and opinions of each citizen to be expressed. Freedom of discussion is not just a safeguard against the abuse of authority but a condition of democracy itself. Equality is important because it recognizes the right of every citizen to be heard. The democratic process, I suggest, is embodied in the detailed implementation of these two principles. Helm (1987, p. 284) put neatly the nub of what has so far been upheld by observing that:

> If people are to be free and equal in the determination of the conditions of their own lives, and enjoy equal rights as well as equal obligations in the specification of the framework which generates and limits the opportunities available to them, they must be in a position to enjoy a range of rights not only in principle, but also in practice.

In a democratic society the implementation of freedom implies that to some extent everybody will care about the welfare and interests of others. There will be a concern that each and every person will be free from fear, molestation and deprivation in the form of such necessities as food, housing and medical aid. There will also be a planned provision in a variety of ways for people to have the freedom to choose, not only between one party and another, or one policy and another, but a pattern of life which is in accord with their own values and interests so long as this does not conflict with the right of others to do the same.

Gould (1990), in keeping with what has been said, argues that freedom in relation to democracy should not be confined to the political or economic spheres, but should include social life and that in particular it is partly to do with a person's self-development. She rightly sees (pp. 40–1) that such characterizing aspects of freedom as the capacity to choose, the absence of constraining conditions and the availability of means, are the preconditions by which a person is not only able to develop his or her own capacities and character but make a contribution to the development of others.

Similarly, such phrases as 'equality of opportunity' and 'consideration for all' are not just pious slogans but are the sentiments upon which the idea of democracy rests. The moral justification of democracy lies in the extent to which the individual person is accorded and given respect. Governments and institutions, if they are to be considered democratic, should be able to meet the test of whether or not they are able to defend their legislative programmes and policies in terms of Kant's (1959, p. 46) imperative: 'Act that you treat humanity in your own person and in the person of everyone else always at the same time as an end and never merely as a means.' What is being invoked here is that in a democratic society the welfare of all people will be equally considered and that no group of people will be deliberately favoured or privileged at the expense of another. A safe rule to follow is that all people or groups of people should be treated the same, unless there are relevant reasons for treating them differently. Few democrats would disagree with the notion, for example, that the poor should have access to legal aid in times of trouble, or that the handicapped should not, in some respects, be treated differently. In a sphere of life such as that of education, for example, treating people with equal consideration may require one group of children being treated differently from another because of such factors as age, aptitude and ability. It is a paradox of equality in a democratic society that in order to bring justice to all, it is sometimes necessary to treat some people differently from others if a respect for their long-term interests is to be borne in mind. Historically, it was Aristotle who first established the principle that it is unjust to treat unequals equally, just as it is unjust to treat equals unequally unless there are valid reasons for doing so.

At the heart of the democratic ideal is the belief that all people, regardless of their colour, race or creed, should be respected, not only because this is desirable in itself, but because they are the centres of consciousness; their distinctive points of view and choice are important to society if it is to remain an open and caring one. What is being suggested then, is that 'respect for persons' is a principle summarizing an attitude that helps identify what it is to be democratic. For a government or institution to treat an individual or group as being unworthy of respect or only as an instrument, is not only to be morally reprehensible but to be undemocratic. Democracy then, is perhaps best understood as a form of society in which respect among members is both given and received. This will be evident in the legislative programmes its government proposes as well as in the procedures by means of which decisions are made.

DEMOCRACY AND EDUCATION

It has been suggested that democracy is more than just a form of government. It is also a socio-cultural, a moral way of life in which persons are free to associate in various ways and express their mature interests and concerns. Certainly, Dewey (1946, p. 28) recognized this latter aspect of democracy. He wrote:

> The keynote of democracy as a way of life may be expressed ... as the necessity for the participation of every mature human being in formation of the values that regulate the living of men together; which is necessary from the standpoint of both the social welfare and the full development of human beings as individuals.

In his *Democracy and Education*, Dewey (1916, p. v) set out to 'detect and state the ideas implied in a democratic society and apply these ideas to the problems and enterprise of education'. He was among the first to show that democracy and education were intimately linked. Dewey saw that if the forthcoming citizens of a democratic society were to play a full part in its deliberations they must learn (a) how to responsibly and effectively participate and (b) to do so preferably with enlightened understanding. Bearing in mind these two requirements the question arises: What form of education is appropriate to a democratic society in which a premium is put upon individual responsibility and community welfare? My answer to this question briefly put is a 'liberal education'. But what is a liberal education and why is this so?

A full answer to each of these questions will not be possible here but an outline sketch will be provided.

Liberal Education

A liberal education is concerned with the liberation of the person who receives it. The classical Greeks saw it as freeing the mind from error and illusion and freeing the person's conduct from wrong-doing. It was the type of education the free man received and is to be contrasted with what is sometimes called vocational training. Traditionally, a liberal education is characterized by its demand for the exercise of a person's intellectual capacities, its apparent non-utilitarian significance, its absence of narrow specialization and intrinsic motivating appeal. More recently Bailey (1984, p. 22) has strikingly exclaimed that: 'A liberal education liberates *from* the tyranny of the present and particular and liberates *for* the ideal of the autonomous, rational, moral agent.'

The paradox of a liberal education is that, although it is concerned with doing things because they are in themselves worthwhile, it has the utilitarian benefit of being of crucial importance in the conduct of everyday affairs. This is because, in developing a knowledge and understanding about the world for its own sake, it will necessarily, in a fundamental sense, prepare people for life and how best to live it.

Peters (1966a, p. 45) in an attempt to provide criteria for what it is to be liberally educated suggests: (1) that it implies the transmission of what is worthwhile; (2) that it must involve knowledge and understanding; and (3) that it rules out some procedures of transmission on the grounds that they lack willingness and voluntariness on the part of the learner.

A liberal education, then, presupposes that it will, in some way, transform an individual for the better; that it gives reason and reasoning a central place; that it only countenances those methods of learning that involve the willing participation of the pupil. Another way of expressing what is being maintained here is by saying that a liberal education is concerned with the initiation of pupils into a worthwhile form of life, particularly with regard to knowledge and understanding in such a way that it is morally defensible. The detailed implications of such a view cannot be embarked upon here. Two strands of it, however, will be picked out and explicated. The first relates to rationality; the second, to morality. It will be seen that both have important implications for citizens in a democratic society.

Rationality

Rationality is usually associated with the idea of enlightened understanding. It is concerned with the giving of reasons, whether in the realm of science or in the realm of human action. To describe an argument as rational is to say something about the process of reasoning involved in it. It is concerned with an attempt to get at the truth of why something occurred, be it to do with an avalanche in the Alps or the death of a neighbour. To provide a rational explanation about an event or instance of conduct does not guarantee its truth but is an attempt to explain something in a reasonable way. Barrow and Woods (1982, p. 83) suggests that:

> A rational argument is . . . one that proceeds logically, that is to say in which each step of the argument as given follows from the preceding step, and in which the reasons that are used to move from the premises to the conclusion are good reasons.

Of greater interest they note that:

> An argument may fall short of being rational in a number of ways: it may refuse to take account of the pertinent evidence that would upset it; it may lay stress on irrelevant evidence; it may appeal to emotion rather than reason; it may contain contradictions and inconsistencies; or it may contain illogical steps.

All in all, it can be said that rationality is a central identifying feature of a liberal education because it places special emphasis on a person's rational capacities and a special belief in the importance of reason and rational argument.

A liberal education, on grounds of the rationality it upholds and aims to cultivate, is of fundamental importance to a democracy for at least two reasons. The first is that sound choices are more likely to be made if they are based on informed judgement and reason rather than upon uninformed opinion, passion or prejudice. The ignorant and gullible are always liable to be more readily exploited and indoctrinated than the educated. Surely, Burke (1774, p. 341) was right when he observed that 'government and legislation are matters of reason and judgement, and not of inclination'. The second reason that a liberal education is of importance to a democracy is that it allows one to see the need for and insist upon the institutionalization of reasoned procedures for the critical and public review of policy. Rationality insists upon accountability for the way in which societal and community affairs are conducted. Rationality, as an inbuilt part of the democratic ideal, insists, as Scheffler (1973, p. 137) put it:

> that judgements of policy be viewed not as the fixed privilege of any class or elite but as the common task of all, and it requires the supplanting of arbitrary and violent alteration of policy with institutionally channelled change ordered by reasoned persuasion and informed consent.

Morality

The second strand of a liberal education that was suggested as having important implications for a democratic society, is that of morality. It is very much connected to the point made earlier about how to participate responsibly and effectively in a democratic society. Without some moral education the citizen may be tempted to act only in his own interests at the expense of the interests of others. If this were the case, such underlying democratic principles as freedom and equality would be at risk and the idea and practice of social justice endangered. It is because a liberal education is inherently concerned with the moral element in life that, in pursuing its own ends, it indirectly serves democracy. What is important to emphasize here is that a liberal education is not a tool of democracy; it is rather a condition for its survival.

What, then, more specifically is morality and moral education? In broad terms it can be said that morality is concerned with our relations with others. It involves our consideration and concern for the welfare of others, as well as for the welfare and interests of ourselves. It is concerned with how to distinguish 'right' from 'wrong' and 'good' from 'bad'. Morality is involved with values and principles to which reference can be made before making a decision or engaging upon a particular course of action. Such principles as universality, impartiality, rational benevolence and liberty are frequently pointed to as underpinning the character of moral discourse and action. Universality and impartiality imply that whatever is recommended by way of prescription should be applicable to all in a fair way. Rational benevolence recognizes the importance of reason giving as well as recognizing the interests of all so that no individual or group is favoured at the expense of another. Liberty brings attention to the point that for an act to be a moral act it must be a free act. That is to say it is a freely chosen act and one for which the agent can be held responsible and accountable.

The term moral education refers to the intentional bringing about of moral growth. It is, according to Kohlberg (1971, p. 25) the encouragement of a capacity for moral judgement. More than this it is also concerned with a disposition to act in accordance with whatever moral judgements are made. What marks out moral education is that it is a deliberate and intentional activity that is concerned with the cultivation of principled moral judgement and a willing disposition to act upon it. Both rational autonomy and strength of will are involved here. To be able to form a moral judgement and yet not act upon it is to fall short of what moral education entails. It is when a moral judgement is translated into an appropriate moral action that moral conduct and therefore moral education is most clearly apparent. McIntosh (1979, p. 167) clearly has something comparable in mind when he writes:

> The morally educated person is expected not only to be able to make moral judgements but act upon them. The moral life necessitates a host of personal dispositions. The moral person must think the issue through to the limits of his capacity, but if morally right action is to occur the person must be disposed to act on his moral judgement.

It should not be thought, in view of what has been said, that moral education is only concerned with the making of moral judgements and the will and capacity to act upon them. In addition to the cognitive and volitional aspects of moral education there is also the affective dimension. To enable children to see that the feelings of other people count as much as their own, requires not only sensitivity but the development of social and practical skills. To recognize that others have feelings like oneself is a matter of knowledge; to regard these feelings as important is an attitude that needs to be cultivated. What, then, is being suggested is that the moral aspect of a liberal education is as much concerned with the emotions as it is with critical judgement and a disposition to act. It will be marked out by an attempt not only to understand a situation with an impartial and sympathetic consideration of the interests at stake but also with a respect for all the persons involved.

At a societal level rather than an inter-personal one moral education in a democracy not only concerns a respect for fellow citizens but the critical appraisal of a state's laws, institutions and policies in accordance with the ideals and principles that underpin and characterize it. Thus Heslep (1989, p. 177) is correct when he argues that 'a moral education befitting a state must give a person the ability to interrelate statements of the principles of voluntary action with statements of the society's laws and other policies'. It is only when the individual exercises his or her rational and moral concerns in a responsible way in the interest of all and holds those in office to be accountable for what they do, is the idea of democracy transformed into a living process.

All in all, it will be seen that a liberal education by virtue of its two inherent central concerns – rationality and morality – is commensurate with the development and survival of the democratic ideal. It does this, not by being an instrument of democracy, but by upholding and pursuing its own values and processes. Liberal education in fulfilling its own purposes also, fortuitously, serves the purposes of democracy.

What, it may be asked, is the sort of person that democracy both needs and wants? Apart from being rational and moral in the way outlined, Gould (1990, pp. 289–94) suggests that such traits as tolerance, reciprocity, mutuality, open mindedness, commitment, responsibility, having initiative and being caring, supportive and communicative are among the most important. It is these same qualities that a liberal education both entails and should help produce. What is being said here should not be confused with or mistaken for the somewhat old-fashioned liberal idea that liberalism is concerned only with the development of autonomous individuals whose mission in life is to seek their own interests and happiness.

THE PLACE OF SPORT IN EDUCATION AND DEMOCRACY

It has been argued that a democracy worthy of its name is dependent upon a liberally educated populace. I will suggest now first, that this traditional view of a liberal education should be updated to include sport; second, that sport is a practice concerned with fairness; and third, that in a democratic state there should be some explicit governmental policy to promote it, especially in the post-school period.

Sport as an Aspect of Liberal Education

It has been maintained that rationality and morality are two central strands in what it means to be liberally educated. While holding to this general position I want to suggest now that rationality can be subdivided into what might be called theoretical rationality and practical rationality. Academic subjects, such as mathematics, science and history would fall into the first category, while sport, dance and other practical pursuits such as cookery and pottery would fall into the second. I want to uphold that a liberal education today should involve an initiation of pupils into the ways, customs, traditions and practices of their society in such a way that it involves both theoretical and practical reasoning and that it should not be confined to one at the expense of the other. Knowing how to engage in such paradigmatic instances of our culture as rugby, soccer, football or cricket is no less an indication of what it is to be liberally educated than is being able to solve quadratic equations or understand Boyle's Law. To see rationality only in theoretical or academic terms is to see it only in terms of thinking *about* the world rather than in terms of acting intelligently *in* it. Practical reasoning, unlike theoretical reasoning, is concerned with practice not theory (or at least not only theory); action, not just thought or belief; intentionally doing something in the world, rather than just thinking or providing information or speculating about the world. Whereas the end of theoretical rationality is universal truth; the end of practical rationality is appropriate action. A contemporary liberal education has as much to do with the latter as it does with the former. Knowing how to participate in a range of worthwhile physical pursuits is an important aspect of human development in that (a) it provides an individual with the opportunity to become a more completely rounded person, and (b) it permits him or her the freedom to choose, in an informed and experienced way, between the inherent values of different types of activity. Overall, the rationality of practical reasoning, especially in reference to sport, permits a range of possibilities in the physical sphere of life to complement those that are primarily intellectual.

In sport, then, not only are thought and action brought together in the agency of the person as he or she confronts what needs to be done in a set of physically demanding and challenging circumstances but, in pursuing a particular activity in a liberal way, the participant is likely to become a more completely developed human being. It will be recalled that MacIntyre (1985, p. 187) points out that sporting practices, as other forms of practices such as chess, farming or engineering, provide opportunities not only for the exercise of particular virtues in the form of justice, honesty, courage and so on, but also for the realization of goods and standards of excellence which 'are appropriate to and partially definitive of that form of activity . . .' He suggests, in keeping with the concept of education, that 'human powers to achieve excellence, and human conceptions of the ends and goods involved are systematically extended'. What is being maintained is that sport, as represented by its various instances, is a socially constituted human practice in which the values inherent in it are realized in the course of trying to achieve the standards of excellence that help characterize it. The 'internal goods' of an activity, as MacIntyre (1985, p. 188) puts it, are so called for two reasons. First, they can only be specified in terms of that activity. Second, they can only be recognized by those who have experienced participating in it.

What then, more specifically, is it that makes practices such as sport valuable to a liberal education? Briefly speaking there are at least four answers that can be given to this question. The first is that they help constitute a meaningful pattern of life in which individuals can both find and extend themselves. It is here that Socrates' phrase 'the unexamined life is not worth living' has significance. Second, they provide the means by which individuals become persons. It is only by being initiated into the ways, customs and practices of a given culture that individuals become the people they are. As Oakshott (1981, pp. 21–2) puts it: 'to be a person is not so much a natural gift but a human achievement'. To be without an understanding of a culture's practices is to be a stranger to the human condition. Third, they are indispensable to moral life for without them there would be little need for the cooperative endeavours and the personal virtues they demand. Practices require people to come together in a state of goodwill in order to pursue common interests and goals. Put in formal terms, people must recognize that it is necessary to abide by the rules and spirit of a practice if its internal goals and standards of excellence are to be realized. Fourth, intrinsically valuable practices like history or chemistry or sport and dance are important to education because they constitute what is worthwhile in a society and should be passed on to the next generation. It will be appreciated too, that if an education is to be liberal it should comprise a selected range of a culture's practices, theoretical and practical, which are then pursued for their own sakes and conducted in a morally defensible way. There is, then, a close relationship between a culture's valued practices and education or an initiation into a balanced range of them. MacIntyre (1964, pp. 19–21) recognizes this when he argues that the proper end of education is 'to help people to discover activities whose ends are not outside themselves. . . . The critical ability which ought to be the fruit of education serves nothing directly except itself, no one except those who exercise it . . . above all the task of education is to teach the value of activity for its own sake'.

Sport as a Practice Concerned with Justice as Fairness

In the light of what has been said, two questions emerge. First, can sport be regarded as having internal goods and, if so, what are they? And second, in what way, if at all, are these goods in keeping with the idea of democracy? Elsewhere[2] I have attempted to give a detailed answer to the former question and so here I shall be mainly concerned with making some brief remarks in relation to the moral aspects of the second question.

The practice of sport, I have argued, as with democracy, is based upon the two principles of freedom and equality. When an individual voluntarily chooses to enter a sport he or she can be regarded as tacitly accepting an agreement with others to participate in a way that the rules[3] lay down. To participate in sport, then, presupposes first, that a free and rational agent has chosen to do so because, in some way, it is found to be valuable; and second, that the agent both understands and is willing to abide by the rules. In broad terms, it will be recalled, the principle of freedom relates to sport in that it assumes that an individual has the right to choose which sport(s) he or she takes up, and in narrow terms by accepting and willingly abiding by the rules that apply to it. To this extent it will be seen that the life and moral character of an individual is bound up and coexistent with the choices made and the activities he or she voluntarily enters into. In this respect, sport is no less serious than other forms of human practice. The point here is that although a sport may be regarded as a particular kind of practice which is characterized and governed by its rules, it is by no means separate from or discontinuous with life or moral concern. In fact, it is an identifiable, if miniature, form of life and not a morally irrelevant one. In so far as sport demands of its participants freedom with responsibility and involves benefits as well as burdens, it is in accord with the democratic process.

The principle of equality, it will also be recalled, relates to sport in that its rules not only structure and shape its practice but are intended to be universal and impartial. Players who are educated in a particular sport come together in the full knowledge that its rules apply to themselves as well as to others. They realize and agree that the rules that apply are in the interests of all players and that it is a part of the expected practice of the sport that they will be objectively applied so that one player or team will not gain unfair advantage over another. It is upon this basis that sport as a competitive practice proceeds. If it were thought that the rules of sport were not concerned with the bringing about of fairness, sport would cease to be the practice it is and should be. It will be seen that the rules that both constitute and govern play should not only be agreed in principle but they should be willingly observed in practice.[4] Those who have grasped the principle of equality as it applies to sport will not only have agreed to willingly abide by a common set of rules and their spirit but will, in addition, understand that it is only by following them that the aspirations and interests of others as well as themselves, as sportsmen or sportswomen, can be realized. Thus, it will be seen that the idea of sport as fairness not only helps preserve its own integrity, standards, traditions and ethos as a distinctive type of human practice, but fortuitously complements what has been said about the nature of education and democracy.

In summary, what I have tried to demonstrate is that democracy as a way of ordering and living our lives is dependent upon the social principles of freedom and equality and that it is these same principles that underpin in turn what it is to be liberally educated as well as the idea of sport as fairness. It is only by an adequate understanding of these principles in relation to these three aspects of life that the latter can be properly understood and safeguarded.

Overall then, it can be said that democracy, education and sport each contribute to the normative structuring of society. Whereas democracy is mainly concerned with the adoption of certain types of procedure that should characterize our political and institutional lives, education is concerned with the initiation of people into those intrinsically worthwhile rational activities, both theoretical and practical, that permit individuals to fulfil their own potential, while at the same time being conscious of and responsible towards the needs and rights of others. Sport relates both to democracy and education in that it is concerned with the exercise of practical knowledge in a physically demanding context in a way that is fair for all. In short, sport should be regarded as a facet of the good life that has its own values, traditions and standards in and through which individuals can fulfil their potentialities and at the same time become more complete and responsible persons. This will not only be of benefit to themselves and to the practice in which they engage but also to the society in which they live.

SPORTS PROVISION AND THE DEMOCRATIC STATE

In so far, then, as a democracy holds that individual responsibility, freedom and equality are desirable in the establishment of a just society it should pursue policies that both protect and promote them. One way of doing this is to make adequate provision not only for education but for sport as one element in the recreative use of leisure time. This would include leadership and amenity planning, as well as financial support.

With the technological revolution that is likely to reduce the average adult working week to no more than four days in the near future, most western democracies recognize that something needs to be done. Few, however, no doubt because of other priorities, have done much on a broad and coherent scale. There is too, in capitalist democracies, the balance of interests to be considered between the public and private sectors and between the commercial and voluntary organizations. Difficult and delicate though this matter may be, the provision of sport in society, on a fair and equitable basis, must remain one of the responsibilities of government. This should not be undertaken, as it has been in the United Kingdom, in response to a general concern about such matters as youth unemployment, delinquency and boredom, but as a matter of citizen rights and the type and quality of a life a modern democratic state should offer. In addition to such well known documented rights[5] as the right to freedom of expression, the right to equality of treatment before the law, the right to education and the right to work, there are other rights, perhaps less well known, but which, in the developed democracies, are becoming increasingly important to implement more fully. These include the right to rest and leisure and the right to take part in cultural life. Sport, I am suggesting, is one aspect of culture for which provision should be made so that it becomes an available option for all citizens who see sport as a part of their individual, social and cultural development.

In the light of what has been said, it is of interest that in 1976 the Council of Europe in a 'Sport for All Charter' set down a number of articles. The first stated that every individual has the right to participate in sport; the second stated that sport shall be encouraged as an important factor in human development and that appropriate support shall be made out of public funds.[6] Although member governments have accepted the principles of the Charter and have made some progress with the eight articles it enumerated, they still have a long way to go in making the slogan live in any fully democratic sense. If further progress is to be made, not only in Europe but elsewhere, it is necessary: (1) that the place of sport in society and the manner in which it is to be conducted should be given a higher priority in the social policy planning of democratic governments; (2) that the inherent values of sport should be more clearly identified and promoted; and (3) that the beneficial outcomes of participation in sport in terms of such considerations as personal health and social welfare should be more comprehensively researched and effectively communicated.

Only when sport is recognized to have intrinsic worth as well as instrumental value, and features more strongly and systematically in education and social policy planning, will it help to bring about the full benefits it is capable of bestowing.

NOTES

1. For much of its long history, from the classical Greeks to modern times, democracy was seen, especially by the educated and enlightened, as one of the worst types of government. It was a term that represented a threat to civilized and law-abiding society. MacPherson (1966, p. 1), for example, comments:

    Democracy used to be a bad word. Everybody who was anybody knew that democracy, in its original sense of rule by the people or government in accordance with the will of the bulk of the people, would be a bad thing – fatal to individual freedom and to all the graces of civilised living. That was the position taken by pretty nearly all men of intelligence from the earliest historical times down to about a hundred years ago. Then, within fifty years, democracy became a good thing.

2. For an attempt to explicate something of the meaning and significance of sport in terms of the experience of the participating agent, see Arnold (1979). For an attempt to spell out the 'internal goods' of sport and dance and relate these to the concept of education, see Arnold (1988).
3. The word 'rules' here is used in a general way and is intended to cover not only the 'formal' rules of sport but also its venerated expectations; that is, its valued traditions, conventions, excellences and shibboleths. For a good discussion on the relationship between the 'formal' rules of a game and the 'ethos' of sport as a social practice, see Morgan (1987).
4. The idea of sport as a practice concerned with fairness is in accord with the way in which Rawls (1972) discusses justice.
5. For a summary of the Major International Human Rights documents, see Winston (1989, pp. 257–89). For a book concerned with an examination of the relationship between human rights and their ethical basis, see Nino (1993).
6. In a later Council of Europe document on sport (1993) it is stated in article 6 that 'The practice of sport, whether it be for the purpose of leisure and recreation, of health promotion, or of improving performance, shall be promoted for all parts of the population through the provision of appropriate facilities and programmes of all kinds and of qualified instructors, leaders or animateurs.'

References

Aristotle (1973) *The Ethics of Aristotle*. Translated by J. A. K. Thompson. London: Penguin.
Aristotle (1985) *Nichomachean Ethics*. Translated by Terence Irwin. Indianapolis: Hackett.
Arnold, P. J. (1979) *Meaning in Movement, Sport and Physical Education*. London: Heinemann.
Arnold, P. J. (1984a) 'Sport, moral education and the development of character', *Journal of the Philosophy of Education*, **18**(2), 275–81.
Arnold, P. J. (1984b) 'Three approaches towards an understanding of sportsmanship', *Journal of the Philosophy of Sport*, **10**, 61–70.
Arnold, P. J. (1988) *Education, Movement and the Curriculum*. London: Falmer Press.
Arnold, P. J. (1989) 'Competitive sport, winning and education', *Journal of Moral Education*, **18**(1), 15–25.
Arnold, P. J. (1991) 'The pre-eminence of skill as an educational value in the school curriculum', *Quest*, **43**(1), 66–77.
Arnold, P. J. (1992) 'Sport as a valued human practice: a basis for the consideration of moral issues in sport', *Journal of the Philosophy of Education*, **26**(1), 237–55.
Arnold, P. J. (1994) 'Sport and moral education', *Journal of Moral Education*, **23**(1), 75–90.
Arnold, P. J. (1996) 'Olympism, sport and education', *Quest*, **48**(1), 93–101.
Aspin, D. (1975) 'Ethical aspects of sports and games', *Proceedings of the Philosophy of Education Society of Great Britain*, **IX** (July), 49–71.
Audi, R. (ed.) (1995) *The Cambridge Dictionary of Philosophy*. Cambridge: Cambridge University Press.
Bailey, C. (1975) 'Games, winning and education', *Cambridge Journal of Education*, **5**(1), 40–50.
Bailey, C. (1984) *Beyond the Present and Particular*. London: Routledge and Kegan Paul.
Barrow, R. and Woods, R. (1982) *An Introduction to Philosophy of Education*. London: Methuen.
Beck, L. W. (1959) *Immanuel Kant: Foundations of the Metaphysics of Morals*. Indianapolis: Bobbs-Merrill.
Bellamy, R. (1982) 'Wilander: a winner and a gentleman', *The Times*, 5 June.
Bigge, M. L. (1982) *Educational Philosophies for Teachers*. Columbus, Ohio: Charles Merrill.
Blum, L. A. (1980) *Friendship, Altruism and Morality*. Boston: Routledge and Kegan Paul.
Blum, L. A. (1994) *Moral Perception and Particularity*. Cambridge: Cambridge University Press.
Borotra, J. (1978) 'A plea for sporting ethics', *Bulletin of the Federation Internationale D'Education Physique*, **48**(3), 7–10.
Boyle, R. N. (1963) *Sport: Mirror of American Life*. Boston: Little Brown and Company.
Brohm, J. M. (1978) *Sport: A Prison of Measured Time*. London: Ink Links.

Brown, W. M. (1980) 'Ethics, drugs and sport', *Journal of the Philosophy of Sport*, **8**, 15–23.
Bullock, A. L. C. (1977) 'Democracy', in A. Bullock and D. Stallybrass (eds), *The Fontana Dictionary of Modern Thought*. London: Fontana Books.
Burke, E. (1774) 'Speech to the Electors of Bristol', 3 November, 1774. Cited in S. I. Benn and R. S. Peters, *Social Principles and the Democratic State*. London: George Allen and Unwin, 1969.
Caillois, R. (1961) *Man, Play and Games*. New York: Free Press of Glencoe.
Carr, D. (1991) *Educating the Virtues*. London: Routledge.
Coakley, J. J. (1986) *Sport in Society: Issues and Controversies*. St Louis: Times Mirror/ Mosby.
Council of Europe (1976) *European Sport for All Charter*, Brussels: Community of Ministers.
Council of Europe (1993) *European Sports Charter*, London: The Sports Council.
Dearden, R. F. (1968) *The Philosophy of Primary Education*. London: Routledge and Kegan Paul.
Dearden, R. F. (1969) 'The Concept of Play', in R. S. Peters (ed.), *The Concept of Education*. London: Routledge and Kegan Paul.
Dearden, R. F. (1976) *Problems in Primary Education*. London: Routledge and Kegan Paul.
Delattre, E. J. (1975) 'Some reflections on success and failure in competitive athletics', *Journal of the Philosophy of Sport*, **2**, 131–9.
Dewey, J. (1916) *Democracy and Education*. New York: Free Press.
Dewey, J. (1946) *The Public and its Problems*. Chicago: Gateway Books.
Dixon, N. (1992) 'On sportsmanship and running up the score', *Journal of the Philosophy of Sport*, **XIX**, 1–13.
Dunlop, F. (1975) 'Bailey on games, winning and education', *Cambridge Journal of Education*, **5**(3) Michaelmas Term, 153–60.
Edwards, H. (1973) *Sociology of Sport*. Homewood, Illinois: The Dorsey Press.
Eitzen, D. S. and Sage, G. H. (1989) *Sociology of North American Sport*. Dubuque, Iowa: W. C. Brown.
Feezell, R. M. (1986) 'Sportsmanship', *Journal of the Philosophy of Sport*, **XII**, 61–70.
Feezell, R. M. (1988) 'On the wrongness of cheating and why cheaters can't play the game', *Journal of the Philosophy of Sport*, **15**, 57–68.
Fielding, M. (1976) 'Against Competition', *Proceedings of the Philosophy of Education Society of Great Britain*, **X** (July), 124–46.
Fraleigh, W. P. (1975) 'Sport-purpose', *Journal of the Philosophy of Sport*, **2**, 74–82.
Fraleigh, W. P. (1982) 'Why the good foul is not good enough', *Journal of Physical Education, Recreation and Dance*, **53** (January), 41–2.
Fraleigh, W. P. (1984) *Right Actions in Sport: Ethics for Contestants*. Champaign, Ill.: Human Kinetics.
Frankena, W. K. (1965) *Three Historical Philosophies of Education*. Glenview, Ill.: Scott Foresman and Company.
Gallie, W. B. (1956) 'Essentially contested concepts', *Proceedings of the Aristotelian Society*, **16**, 167–98.
Gallie, W. B. (1964) *Philosophy and Historical Understanding*. London: Chatto and Windus.
Gardner, R. (1989) 'On performance enhancing substances and the unfair advantage argument', *Journal of the Philosophy of Sport*, **16**, 59–73.
Gert, B. (1988) *Morality: A New Justification of the Moral Rules*. Oxford: Oxford University Press.
Gibson, J. H. (1993) *Performance Versus Results: A Critique of Values in Contemporary Sport*. Albany, New York: State University of New York Press.
Gilligan, C. (1982) *In a Different Voice: Psychological Theory and Women's Development*. Cambridge, Mass.: Harvard University Press.
Gough, R. W. (1995) 'On reaching first base with a "science" of sport ethics: problems with scientific objectivity and reductivism', *Journal of the Philosophy of Sport*, **13**, 11–25.
Gould, C. C. (1990) *Rethinking Democracy: Freedom and Cooperation in Politics, Economy and Society*. Cambridge: Cambridge University Press.
Graves, H. (1900) 'A philosophy of sport', *The Contemporary Review*, **LXXVIII** (Dec), 877–93.

Grayham, P. J. and Ueberhorst, H. (1976) *The Modern Olympics*. West Point, NY: Leisure Press.

Grice, G. R. (1967) *The Ground of Moral Judgement*. New York: Cambridge University Press, chapter 4.

Hare, R. M. (1981) *Moral Thinking*. Oxford: Clarendon Press.

Harper, W. (1993) 'Just sport', *Quest*, **45**, 448–59.

Hart, H. L. A. (1975) 'Are there any natural rights?', *Philosophy Review*, **64**, (April). Cited in Simmons (1979).

Helm, D. (1987) *Models of Democracy*. Cambridge: Polity Press.

Hersh, R. H., Miller, J. P. and Fielding, D. (1980) *Models of Moral Education: An Appraisal*. New York: Longman.

Heslep, R. D. (1989) *Education in Democracy*. Iowa: Iowa State University Press.

Hirst, P. H. and Peters, R. S. (1970) *The Logic of Education*. London: Routledge and Kegan Paul.

Hirst, P. H. (1993) 'Education, knowledge and practices', in R. Barrow and P. White (eds), *Beyond Liberal Education. Essays in Honour of Paul Hirst*. London: Routledge.

Hoch, P. (1972) *Rip Off the Big Game: The Explanation of Sports by the Power Elite*. New York: Doubleday, Archer Books.

Horton, J. and Mendus, S. (1994) *After MacIntyre*. Cambridge: Polity Press.

Hospers, J. (1990) *An Introduction to Philosophical Analysis*. London: Routledge.

Huizinga, J. (1970) *Homo Ludens, A Study of the Play Element in Culture*. London: Paladin Press.

Hussey, M. M. (1938) 'Character education in athletics', *The American Educational Review*, (November), 578–80.

Huxley, A. (1969) *Ends and Means*. London: Chatto and Windus.

Hyland, D. A. (1990) *Philosophy of Sport*. New York: Paragon House.

International Olympic Committee (1994) *Olympic Charter*.

Jones, J. G. and Pooley, J. C. (1982) 'Cheating in sport: an international problem', *International Journal of Physical Education*, **3**, 19–23.

Kant, E. (1959) *Foundations of the Metaphysics of Morals*. Translated by L. W. Beck. Indianapolis: Bobbs-Merrill.

Kant, E. (1991) *Education*. Translated by G. A. Churton. Ann Arbor: University of Michigan Press.

Keating, J. W. (1973) 'The ethics of competition and its relation to some moral problems in athletics', in R. G. Osterhoudt (ed.), *The Philosophy of Sport*. Springfield, Ill.: Charles C. Thomas.

Keating, J. W. (1979) 'Sportsmanship as a moral category', in E. W. Gerber and W. J. Morgan (eds), *Sport and the Body*, 2nd edn. Philadelphia: Lea and Febiger.

Keating, J. W. (1988) 'Sportsmanship as a moral category', in W. J. Morgan and K. V. Meier (eds), *Philosophic Enquiry in Sport*. Champaign, Ill.: Human Kinetics.

Keenan, F. W. (1975) 'Justice and sport', *Journal of the Philosophy of Sport*, **2**, 115–19.

Kew, F. C. (1978) 'Values in competitive games', *Quest*, **29**, 103–13.

Kitson Clark, G. (1962) *The Making of Victorian England*. London: Methuen.

Kleiber, D. A. and Roberts, G. C. (1981) 'The effects of sport experience in the development of social character: an exploratory investigation', *Journal of Sport Psychology*, **3**, 114–22.

Kohlberg, L. (1971) 'Stages of moral development as a basis for moral education', in C. M. Beck, B. S. Crittenden and E. S. Sullivan (eds), *Moral Education – Interdisciplinary Approaches*. Toronto: University of Toronto Press, pp. 30–41.

Kohn, A. (1986) *No Contest. The Case Against Competition*. Boston: Houghton Mifflin.

Kolnai, A. (1966) 'Games and aims', *Proceedings of the Aristotelian Society*, 103–8.

Kretchmar, R. S. (1994) *Practical Philosophy of Sport*. Champaign, Ill.: Human Kinetics.

Lasch, C. (1979) *The Culture of Narcissism: American Life in an Age of Diminished Expectations*. New York: Warner.

Leamon, O. (1988) 'Cheating and fair play in sport', in W. Morgan and K. Meier (eds), *Philosophic Enquiry in Sport*. Champaign, Ill.: Human Kinetics, pp. 277–82.

Lehman, C. K. (1981) 'Can cheaters play the game?', *Journal of the Philosophy of Sport*, **8**, 41–6.

Leonard, W. M. (1993) *A Sociological Perspective of Sport*. New York: Macmillan.

Lickona, T. (1992) *Educating for Character*. London: Bantam Books.

Loland, S. (1995) 'Coubertin's ideology of Olympism from the perspective of the history of ideas', *Olympica*, **4**, 49–78.

Loy, J. W. (1969) 'The nature of sport: a definitional effort', in J. W. Loy and G. S. Kenyon (eds), *Sport, Culture and Society*. London: Collier – Macmillan, pp. 56–71.

Lucas, J. R. (1959) 'Moralists and gamesmen', *Philosophy*, **34**(11), 1–11.

Lumpkin, A., Stoll, S. K. and Beller, J. M. (1994) *Sport Ethics: Applications for Fair Play*. St Louis, Mo.: Mosby.

Lyons, N. P. (1983) 'Two perspectives: on self, relationships and morality', *Harvard Educational Review*, **53**, 125–45.

McIntosh, P. (1979) *Fair Play: Ethics in Sport and Education*. London: Heinemann.

MacIntyre, A. (1964) 'Against utilitarianism', in Hollins, T. H. B. (ed.), *Aims in Education*. Manchester: Manchester University Press.

MacIntyre, A. (1971) *Against the Self Images of the Age*. London: Duckworth.

MacIntyre, A. C. (1984) 'Is patriotism a virtue?', The Lindley Lecture, p. 10. University of Kansas.

MacIntyre, A. C. (1985) *After Virtue: A Study in Moral Theory*. London: Duckworth.

MacIntyre, A. C. (1988) *Whose Justice? Which Rationality?* London: Duckworth.

MacIntyre, A. C. (1990) *Three Rival Versions of Moral Enquiry: Encyclopaedia, Genealogy, Tradition*. London: Duckworth.

McNamee, M. (1995) 'Sporting practices, institutions and virtues: a critique and a restatement', *Journal of the Philosophy of Sport*, **32**, 61–82.

MacPherson, C. B. (1966) *The Real World of Democracy*. Oxford: Clarendon Press.

Mangan, J. A. (1975) 'Athleticism: a case study of the evaluation of an educational ideology', in B. Simon and I. Bradley (eds), *The Victorian Public School*. London: Gill and Macmillan.

Mangan, J. A. (1981) *Athleticism in the Victorian and Edwardian Public School*. London: Falmer Press.

Maraj, J. A. (1965) 'Physical education and character', *Education Review*, **17**(2) (February), 103–13.

Meakin, D. C. (1981) 'Physical education: an agency of moral education?', *Journal of the Philosophy of Education*, **15**(2), 241–53.

Meakin, D. C. (1982) 'Moral values and physical education', *Physical Education Review*, **5**(1), 62–82.

Meakin, D. C. (1986) 'The moral status of competition', *Journal of the Philosophy of Education*, **20**(1), 59–67.

Meier, K. V. (1981) 'On the inadequacies of a sociological definition of sport', *International Review of Sport Sociology*, **16**(2), 79–100.

Meier, K. V. (1988) 'Triad trickery: playing with sport and games', *Journal of the Philosophy of Sport*, **15**, 11–30.

Meier, K. V. (1993) 'Amateurism and the nature of sport', *Quest*, **45**, 494–509.

Melden, A. I. (1980) *Rights and Persons*. Berkeley: University of California Press.

Messner, J. (1990) 'When bodies are weapons: masculinity and violence in sport', *International Review of the Sociology of Sport*, **25**, 3.

Midgley, M. (1974) 'The game game', *Philosophy*, **49**, 231–53.

The Miller Lite Report on American Attitudes to Sport (1983) Milwaukee, Wis.: Miller Brewing Company.

Morgan, W. J. (1987) 'The logical incompatibility thesis and rules: a reconsideration of formalism' as an Account of Games, *Journal of the Philosophy of Sport*, **14**, 1–20.

Morgan, W. J. (1993) 'Amateurism and professionalism as moral languages in search of a moral image for sport', *Quest*, **45**, 470–93.

Morgan, W. J. (1994) *Leftist Theories of Sport: A Critique and Reconstruction*. Urbana: University of Illinois Press.

Morgan, W. J. and Meier, K. V. (eds) (1988) *Philosophic Enquiry in Sport*. Champaign, Ill.: Human Kinetics.

Morris, S. (ed.) (1979) *The Book of Strange Facts and Useless Information*. New York: Dolskin.
Nino, C. S. (1993) *The Ethics of Human Rights*. Oxford: Clarendon Press.
Nisbet, S. (1972) *Purpose in the Curriculum*. London: University of London Press.
Noddings, N. (1984) *Caring: A Feminine Approach to Ethics and Moral Education*. Berkeley, Calif.: University of California Press.
Oakshott, M. (1981) 'Education: the engagement and its frustration', in R. F. Dearden, P. H. Hirst and R. S. Peters (eds), *Education and the Development of Reason*. London: Routledge and Kegan Paul.
Ogilvie, B. C. and Tutko, A. T. (1971) 'Sport: if you want to build character try something else', *Psychology Today*, (October) **5**, 61–3.
Olympic Rules and Regulations (1974) Lausanne: International Olympic Committee.
Osterhoudt, R. G. (ed.) (1973) *The Philosophy of Sport*, Springfield, Ill.: Thomas.
Osterhoudt, R. G. (1990) *The Philosophy of Sport*. Champaign, Ill.: Stipes Publishing Company.
Perry, L. R. (1975) 'Competition and co-operation', *British Journal of Educational Studies*, **XXIII**(2) (June), 127–34.
Peters, R. S. (1966a) *Ethics and Education*. London: Allen and Unwin.
Peters, R. S. (1966b) 'Moral education and the psychology of character', in I. Scheffler (ed.), *Philosophy and Education*, 2nd edn, Boston: Allyn and Bacon.
Peters, R. S. (1972) *Reason and Compassion*. London: Routledge and Kegan Paul.
Peters, R. S. (1981) *Moral Development and Moral Education*. London: George Allen and Unwin.
Plato (1955) *The Republic*. Translated by H. D. P. Lee. Harmondsworth: Penguin.
Pojman, L. P. (1995) 'Relativism', in Audi, R. (ed.), *The Cambridge Dictionary of Philosophy*. Cambridge: Cambridge University Press, pp. 690–1.
Pring, R. (1984) *Personal and Social Education in the Curriculum*. London: Hodder and Stoughton.
Prvulovich, Z. R. (1982) 'In defence of competition', *Journal of Philosophy of Education*, **16**(1), 77–88.
Quinton, A. (1982) *Thoughts and Thinkers*. New York: Holmes and Meier.
Rawls, J. (1958) 'Justice as fairness', *The Philosophy Review*, **LXVII**(2) (April), 164–94.
Rawls, J. (1973) *A Theory of Justice*. New York: Oxford University Press.
Rosenburg, D. (1993) 'Sportsmanship reconsidered', *International Journal of Physical Education*, **30**(2), 15–23.
Rosenburg, D. (1995) 'The concept of cheating in sport', *International Journal of Physical Education*, **32**(2), 4–14.
Rousseau, J. J. (1974) *Emile*. Translated by B. Foxley. London: J. M. Dent.
Ryle, G. (1975) 'Can virtue be taught?', in R. F. Dearden, P. H. Hirst and R. S. Peters (eds), *Education and Reason*. London: Routledge and Kegan Paul.
Scheffler, I. (1973) *Reason and Teaching*. London: Routledge and Kegan Paul.
Schmitz, K. L. (1979) 'Sport and play: suspension of the ordinary', in E. W. Gerber and W. J. Morgan (eds), *Sport and the Body*, 2nd edn. Philadelphia: Lea and Febiger.
Schneider, A. J. and Butcher, R. B. (1993) 'For the love of the game', *Quest*, **45**, 460–9.
Schneider, A. J. and Butcher, R. B. (1993/4) 'Why olympic athletes should avoid the use and seek the elimination of performance enhancing substances and practices from the olympic games', *Journal of the Philosophy of Sport*, **20/21**, 64–8.
Scott, J. (1973) 'Sport and the radical ethic', *Quest*, **19**, 71–7.
Shea, E. J. (1978) *Ethical Decisions in Physical Education and Sport*. Springfield, Ill.: C. Thomas.
Shields, D. L. and Bredemeier, B. J. (1994) *Character Development and Physical Activity*. Champaign, Ill.: Human Kinetics.
Shirley, W. (1983) 'Is it really a sin to lose?', *The Denver Post*, 11 November, D1.
Simmons, A. J. (1979) 'The principle of fair play', *Philosophy and Public Affairs*, **8**(4)(Summer).
Simon, R. L. (1985) *Sport and Social Values*. Englewood Cliffs, NJ: Prentice Hall.
Simon, R. L. (1991) *Fair Play: Sports, Values and Society*. Boulder, CA and Oxford: Westview Press.

Singer, P. (ed.) (1994) *A Companion to Ethics*. Oxford: Basil Blackwell.
Smith, R. (1993) 'History of amateurism in men's intercollegiate athletics: the continuance of a 19th century anachronism in athletics'. *Quest*, **45**, 430–97.
Solomon, R. C. (1984) *Ethics: A Brief Introduction*. New York: McGraw-Hill.
'A Sportsmanship Brotherhood' (1926) *Literary Digest*, **88** (27 March), p. 60.
Suits, B. (1988) 'Tricky triad: games, play and sport', *Journal of the Philosophy of Sport*, **15**, 1–9.
Sullivan R. J. (1994) *Introduction to Kant's Ethics*. Cambridge: Cambridge University Press.
Thiroux, J. P. (1990) *Ethics: Theory and Practice*. New York: Macmillan Publishing Company.
Thomas, C. E. (1983) *Sport in a Philosophic Context*. Philadelphia: Lea and Febiger.
Thompson, K. (1975) 'The point of an activity', *Cambridge Journal of Education*, **5**(3) (Michaelmas Term).
Uppingham Magazine (1972) **10** (April), 72.
Urmson, J. O. (1958) 'Saints and heroes', in A. I. Melden (ed.), *Essays in Moral Philosophy*. Seattle: University of Washington Press.
Urmson, J. O. (1988) *Aristotle's Ethics*. Oxford: Blackwell.
Vanderwerken, D. L. and Wertz, S. K. (1985) *Sport Inside Out*. Fort Worth: Texas Christian University.
Warnock, M. (1977) *Schools of Thought*. London: Faber and Faber.
Weiss, M. R. and Bredemeier, B. J. (1986) 'Moral development', in V. Seefeldt (ed.), *Physical Activity and Well-being*. Reston, Va.: American Association for Health, Physical Education, Recreation and Dance.
Weiss, P. (1969) *Sport: A Philosophic Enquiry*. Carbondale: Southern Illinois University Press.
White, J. P. (1982) *The Aims of Education Restated*. London: Routledge and Kegan Paul.
Wigmore, S. and Tuxill, C. (1995) 'A consideration of the concept of fair play'. *European Physical Education Review*, **1**(1), 67–73.
Will, G. F. (1985) 'Exploring the racer's edge', *News Week*, 4 February, 88.
Williams, B. (1976) 'Persons, character and morality', in A. O. Rorty (ed.), *The Identity of Persons*. Berkeley: University of California Press.
Wilson, J. (1966) *Equality*. London: Hutchinson.
Wilson, J. (1971) *Moral Thinking*. London: Heinemann.
Wilson, J. (1986) 'Competition', *The Journal of Moral Education*, **18**(1), 26–31.
Winston, M. E. (1989) *The Philosophy of Human Rights*. Belmont, Calif.: Wadsworth Publishing Company.
Wright, D. (1971) *The Psychology of Moral Behaviour*. Harmondsworth: Penguin.

Name Index

Subject Index